W9-DGH-339

RELIGIOUS VALUES

IN

JAPANESE CULTURE

T. T. Brumbaugh, S.T.M.

KYO BUN KWAN

(Christian Literature Society of Japan)

TOKYO

1934

CHINESE-JAPANESE LIBRARY
HARVARD-YENCHING INSTITUTE
AT HARVARD UNIVERSITY

JUN 30 1949

W1760/09 c.2

War Dep't

TO

MY WIFE

FOREWORD

Events in the Far East since the opening of the present century, and in particular since the beginning of the World War, have concentrated the attention of Western peoples upon that small but energetic island empire, Japan. This is because Japan has within such an amazingly brief period of modern history evolved from the chrysalis of isolated medievalism to recognition as one of the great nations of the world and now presumes to assume the leadership of the entire Orient in culture and in prowess.

To comprehend this phenomenon and to properly appraise its significance European and American people are now seeking to acqaint themselves with the Japanese and their cultural background. That Japan's cultural tradition is essentially religious is one of any student's earliest discoveries. Contrary to certain popular conceptions, delving into either the history of Japan or the psychological make-up of its people today discloses the inescapable fact that the Japanese are, as one has said of man in general, "incurably religious." It is therefore obvious that a fair and honest appraisal of the religious values of Japanese culture is essential

both for insight into present conditions in Japan
and for any trustworthy forecast of the probable
course of development in future.

There is much of permanent value in the religious
culture of Japan, and it is to promote such an appreciation of these eternal "goods" as will en-
courage Western peoples in their relations with the
Japanese to build upon rather than to destroy these
goodly foundations, that the writer has been led to
put forth in book form the study herein submitted.
It is his hope that emphasis upon the noble and
worth-full, rather than upon the undesirable and
base, may inspire larger confidence in the ideals
and motives of the Japanese people, and in turn
call forth from them greater devotion to the principles of goodness, beauty and truth which are implicit in their own indigenous culture. Such an
approach to Japanese psychology, I am convinced,
will accomplish far more in helping to realize the
Christ-like ideals of justice, love and peace in the
Orient than the employment of iconoclastic methods
either in evangelizing a proud and cultured nation
or in reproving its people for sins which all sturdy
races have in times past—and not too far past
among the white peoples of the earth—been guilty.

For assistance in securing and arranging the
materials for this study I wish to acknowledge my
indebtedness to Professors Robert E. Hume and
Daniel J. Fleming, and others, at Union Theological

Seminary in New York. For reading the manuscript and for many valuable suggestions I am especially grateful to Dr. M. Anesaki and his colleagues in the Department of the Science of Religions at Tokyo Imperial University; also to Dr. A. K. Reischauer of the Woman's Christian College in Japan, and to Dr. S. H. Wainright of the Christian Literature Society in Tokyo. There are many other debts of gratitude too numerous to mention, but if the book accomplishes to some degree the author's purpose there may be in this some remuneration for all those who have had a share in bringing him to his present high regard for the virtues of the Japanese people and his deep-seated desire to help them achieve their rightful place in that "One family under Heaven" of which the Japanese have been taught by Confucius, Buddha and Christ.

—T. T. B.

Tokyo, Japan.
February 1, 1934.

OUTLINE

f. Indwelling Presence urging to cooperation with the Divine.

g. The place of Jesus Christ in the religious life of Japan today.

CONCLUSION   pp. 125–139

a. The *Church* may fail in Japan, but *Christ*-ianity will triumph.

b. Historically Christianity has recognized values in other cultures.

c. Both encouragement and warning in story of Buddhism's adaptation.

d. A religion may adapt itself to meet different cultural conditions, Dr. Ernst Troeltsch to the contrary notwithstanding.

e. Japan's culture, in conforming to the best in Western civilization, needs new moral and religious vigor.

f. Test for Christianity lies in ability to integrate itself with Japanese life.

g. Need of a homiletic peculiarly fitted for the Japanese people.

h. Missionaries' concern only with Fatherhood of God and Brotherhood of Men, in which other religions are passive or negative.

i. The tree of Japanese culture—its fruit wholesome, though like the persimmon.

j. The Religion of the Future in Japan—following Professor W. E. Hocking's suggestions.

k. An attempt to picture the Ideal for the Japanese: Values transmitted from the past, plus one's own feeling for God, the sense of one's own and each other's worth, belief in the future life, and the *desire for perfection*.

l. From Japan's *Old* Testament to the writing of the *New*.

INTRODUCTION

The religious culture of Japan is a tapestry woven from strands of tradition both native and foreign to the country first referred to as the "Central Land of the Reed Plains."[-1] Even a superficial examination of Japanese thought and life today will disclose several of the most significant of these strands of influence :

a. Native primitive animism ;
b. Polytheism, and the differentiation of celestial deities ;
c. Chinese culture, including, Confucian and Taoist elements ;
d. Buddhism, particularly the Mahayana ;
e. Confucianism as a philosophy of morals ;
f. Shinto, as developed in modern times ;
g. Christianity, following both early Catholic and modern missionary contacts.

These developments in chronological order of appearance in Japan, with the inclusion of that peculiar medieval phenomenon resulting from the fusion of Buddhism with the native religious beliefs and known as *Ryobu-Shinto* (i.e. The Two-fold Way of the Gods) to distinguish it from *Butsudo* (The

Way of Buddha), and with a later word about
Modern Buddhism, constitute the background out
of which the writer proposes to draw to attention
certain elements of genuine and permanent value
in the religious culture of Japan,—elements which
most students of that culture admit to be inherent
in it ; values that should be taken into account by
any religious teacher or reformer who seeks to
promote a more advanced moral and religious consciousness among the Japanese people.

I. NATIVE PRIMITIVE ANIMISM

For any adequate comprehension of the origins of present day Japanese history and character one must give large attention to that most primitive period of the religion of Nippon, dating back before the opening of the Christian era we know not how long, but an age when men lived utterly untutored lives and worshipped the very things upon which barest existence depended: "birds, beasts, plants and trees, seas and mountains, and all other things whatsoever which deserve to be dreaded and revered for the extraordinary powers which they possess,"[1] i.e. things having "isao", power or virtue.[2]

Of this era there is no literature extant and only the slightest archeological data. Perhaps it harks back to the age of the *Korupo Unguri*, whom Dr. Inazo Nitobe mentions as the true aborigines of Japan.[3] Neither Brinkley nor Murdock, two of the earliest compilers of critical histories of the Japanese people, nor Professor Anesaki, one of the greatest living authorities on Japanese religious history, advances any information about the stock of which Dr.

Nitobe speaks. About all we can be sure of is that, whoever first occupied the islands of Japan in these primeval ages and prior to the arrival of the peoples who later came to constitute the so-called *Yamato* race, much of the main island now known as Hondo was held and inhabited by a non-Mongolian people called *Ainu*, several thousands of whom still live in northern Japan. Further, it is safe to say that these primitives, and any others who may have stood in the path of the more pigmented invading hosts from the south and west, were a contributing factor in the cultural and religious life of the conquerors. It seems certain, for instance, that the name of Japan's sacred mountain, *Fuji*, came from a form of Ainu fire-worship conducted on its slopes.[4] We are also aware that even to this day the Ainu worship the bear, not the spirit of the bear but the bear itself, which they kill and eat that they may appropriate the animal's courage and strength.[5]

A. AWE AND REVERENCE IN THE PRESENCE OF NATURE

In such pure animism it may seem to some that there can be little to recognize as of genuine religious value. Yet there was in this earliest period of Japanese history that without which there can be no religion whatsoever; we refer to a sentiment of awe in the presence of

Nature. Moreover, there was something more than mere awe, which is often nothing other than fear when confronted by mighty natural forces; here in Japan, however, it is a friendly relationship with and reverence for Nature which has ever characterized the native religious spirit of the people and has been such a dominant factor in their cultural life.[5] Peculiarly, the Japanese, who perhaps have had more reason to fear the forces that produce earthquakes, fire, storm, flood, and other natural disasters, are less given to the fear-complex than many peoples more fortunately situated. Instead, the awesome aspects of nature upon which they are so dependent seem to have brought to the Japanese a sense of their oneness with all that makes up their environment. It is a patent observation concerning the Japanese that "probably in no other portion of the earth are the people and the land more like each other or apparently better acquainted."[6] And this has made religion such a natural part of the experience and dreams of these primitive peoples that fact and fancy are almost inextricably associated. Prof. G. W. Knox asks the rhetorical question, "In a world which as yet knew no distinction between man and beast, or man and and God, where matter and spirit were no separate categories, how should one distinguish between history and romance?"[7]

We may therefore say that the distinguishing
religious feature of this early period of Japanese life was a wholesome sentiment of awe and
reverence, which in turn induced the desire for
worship, for prayer, and for communion with
Nature.[8] This I would also single out as the
most fundamental aspect of the religious culture of Japan today.   It may be an Oriental, it
may be a universal, human trait; at least it is a
genuine characteristic of the Japanese that they
are reverent in the presence of phenomena not
comprehended and greater than themselves. It
was perfectly natural, therefore, that a Japanese student's definition of religion, given the
writer some time ago in reply to a questionnaire,
should approach the subject first from a rever-
ential viewpoint: "Religion is that attitude toward the universe which, whether with or without supernatural aid, pours into life the spirit of
reverence, and . . . . ." The remainder of the
definition, not germane here, will appear in its
appropriate time; but this much indicates how
truly awe and reverence form an integral part
in the religious consciousness of Japan, mores
harking back to antiquity when animism was
the sole religion of a primitive people. Of these
rudiments of religion, Professor Knox has aptly
said: "It is not superstition, nor is it mere custom, nor is it simply the arousing of the æsthet-
ic nature. It is the beginning of religion, adora-

tion and dependence, praise and prayer, faith and rite; not knowing what it is, but only that in the soul there is a sense of a greater than self which we joy to worship, a more powerful than self on which we must depend."[9] This is, indeed, one of the most universal and value-full elements in religion, and the Japanese are fortunate to have so early felt and embraced it.

II. POLYTHEISM, AND THE DIFFEREN-
TIATION OF CELESTIAL DEITIES

Sometime, perhaps about the dawn of the Christian era, there came to that part of Japan which became the cradle of her later culture one or more strains of foreign blood; which, when fused with that of the people already there, came to constitute the Japanese race, a composite people yet peculiarly fitted to forge through the centuries that distinctive culture and social unity well known to the world today as Japanese civilization.[1] Among these invading tribes or hordes there was one which, either alone or in fusion with other strains of blood, came to be known as the *Yamato* people, and among whom a great leader appeared, destined to be recognized as Japan's first emperor, the celebrated Jimmu Tenno. It was probably he who first reduced the land and its mixture of peoples to a semblance of unity, subduing all opposition and civil strife. And, whence-so-ever its origin, it was the Yamato race, doubtless, which brought to acceptance throughout Japan a conception of deity more exalted than merely an object powerful and uncomprehended.

Certain it is that at some time long prior to the eighth century A.D. there arose in Japan a belief in gods as divorced from things, gods resembling in many ways those of the Greek pantheon and regarded as engaging in purposeful and creative activities, from which emerged the Central Land of the Reed Plains and all that was therein. Some of these highly mythological conceptions are preserved for our study in two early efforts at history written in Chinese characters, the *Kojiki* (Records of Ancient Matters), and the *Nihongi* (Chronicles of Japan), dating from 712 and 720 A.D. respectively. It is not in the province of this paper to treat of these sources extensively, yet it may be observed by way of substantiating our thesis that in the Kojiki and the Nihongi there is distinct evidence of polytheistic mythology superimposed upon a more primitive animistic religious ideology,[2] very much as we become aware of a similar ingraftation in the Old Testament when Cain, supposedly the first son of the first man created upon the earth, goes off to the land of Nod and takes a wife, rears children and builds a city.[3]

The Kojiki, for example, begins by accounting for the host of celestial deities which are obviously super-mundane: Master-of-the-August-Center-of-Heaven, High-August-Producing-Wondrous-Deity, etc. (I. i) Following this there appear numerous deities that might be associated with an earthly function but are nevertheless celestial beings: e.g. Earthly-Eternally-Standing-Deity, Germ-Integrating-Deity, the Male-Who-Invites, and the Female-Who-Invites (I.ii). Thereupon the two latter—in Japanese *Izanagi* and *Izanami*—set out to create land from the Floating Bridge of Heaven (I. iii-v). Eventually are created the nature deities Rock-Earth-Prince, Heavenly-Blowing-Male, Sea-Deity, etc. etc. (I.vi,x). This is of course in somewhat the same order as the Genesis story of creation, but surely reflects an historical evolution of thought in the reverse order: all we know of earliest Japanese culture points to acquaintance with the earthly deities before differentiating the celestial order here given first in order of appearance.

Again, a little later we read of the birth of the Heaven-Illumining-August-Deity or Sun-Goddess (*Ama-terasu O-mikami*), the Moon-Ruler, and then of the impetuous god *Susa-no-wo*, brother of the Sun-Goddess and deity of the Wind, who when expelled from the Plain of High Heaven came down to the Land of Idzumo, found "people at the headwaters of the river," and took his wife therefrom after killing a dreadful "eight-forked serpent" which was preying upon the daughters of the land (Kojiki I.xviii). Thereupon Susa-no-wo and his bride set about begetting earthly gods: Great-Harvest-Deity, August-Spirit-of-Food, Great-Water-Master, etc. (I.xx), and eventually Deity-Master-of-the-Great-Land (*Okuni-nushi-no-mikoto*), who becomes the supreme deity of the land of Idzumo but is cajolled into abdicating sovereignty over practical affairs in favor of the August Grandson of the Sun-Goddess when this one of higher authority is sent to claim the Central Land of the Reed Plains for the gods of the Plain of High Heaven (I.xxx-xxxiii).

Here is ample testimony to the existence of two, and probably three or more strata of religious mythology, the nominal triumph of the more highly evolved polytheism of the conquerors, yet the interpenetration of the nobler with the cruder conception of the more primitive peoples.[4] It would be difficult today to classify these deities accurately in categories of clearly distinguished nature gods on the one hand and those of celestial realm on the other—perhaps there never was such a clear demarcation. But obviously the gods of the Plain of High Heaven are of an order different from, also higher and later than, the earliest nature gods to whom we have been introduced. Dr. Aston regards Izanagi and Izanami and their celestial ilk as perhaps unconscious echoes of the Yin and the Yang of Chinese philosophy.[5] Be that as it may, while it may not be correct to say that Japan's deities had as yet been genuinely personalized

—although in some instances this conclusion seems justified—at least they had been to a degree spiritualized, and *Kami*, instead of connoting merely a thing higher and more powerful than man, and hence to be designated by the Chinese character for "higher" 上, came to mean that which was different, sublime, divine, for which the ideograph 神 had to be used.[6]

A. "FILIAL FAMILIARITY" WITH, GRATITUDE AND LOVE TOWARD, A HIGHER ORDER OF KAMI

While this newer conception of deity was, as Prof. Genchi Kato points out, an "unequivocal polytheism,[7] and as such marks a distinct advance over the purely animistic concepts of an earlier age, nevertheless it is significant that in the change none of the old "filial familiarity" with the *Kami* was lost.[8] The sublimated *Kami* seem never to have become so holy or so awesome as to divorce themselves from the lives of their worshippers. "As Heaven, earth, Hades, and the world beneath the sea are all of a kind, and one may abide indifferently in any, so is there no real difference in their inhabitants," says Knox.[9] Even Hades has its pleasant abodes and peaceful plains (Kojiki I.xxiii). What wonder then that, as Aston exclaims ardently, "Shinto is a religion of gratitude and love. The great gods, such as the Sun Goddess and the Deity of Food, are beneficent beings. They are addressed as parents, or dear divine ancestors, and their festivals have a joyous character.[10] A blessed fellowship this, and one that should be preserved if religion is to be a natural and happy experience of the heart. Here is an abiding value in the religious consciousness of Japan: since time immemorial the Japanese have felt the bonds of actual fellowship and love with their celestial progenitors; and the credulous still derive that satisfaction from their faith.

B. AN IMPOSED RESPONSIBILITY—FORMAL PURITY AND THE BEGINNINGS OF MORALITY.

It must not be assumed, as is sometimes avowed, that a beneficent interpretation of the divine imposes slight responsibilities. Rather does it seem reasonable that where the implications of love are understood a child should feel himself under greater obligation to a loving than to a cruel parent. That there was some appreciation of the responsibility imposed through kinship with the deities even in this primitive Japanese society seems obvious. Even the gods appear under the compulsion of at least formal rectitude. *Izanagi*, when he returns from his visit to Hades, must wash himself "with repeated washings."[11] Thus purification becomes an obligation upon all conscious life; a primitive and formal purification, to be sure,

but involving prayers and gifts and desire for
closer fellowship with the divine, and destined
to take on ethical content as generations pass,
until there comes to be real moral significance
in the statement of a priest that "If Shinto has
one dogma, it is purity."[12]

Moreover, there is evidence in both the Kojiki (I.xv, xvii) and the Nihongi (I.37-48) of a
beginning of every-day morality which these
primitives so identified with the universal order
as to be imposed upon the gods themselves. We
read also in the *Yengishiki*, a book dating from
the tenth century but describing and illustrating
ceremonies inaugurated in a far earlier age,
that

> "of the various faults and transgressions to be
> committed by the celestial race destined more
> and more to people this land of his peaceful
> rule, some are of Heaven, to wit, the break-
> ing down of divisions between rice fields, fill-
> ing up irrigation channels, removing water-
> pipes, sowing seed over again, planting skew-
> ers, flaying alive, flaying backwards . . . . .
> Earthly offences which will be committed
> are the cutting of living bodies, the cutting of
> dead bodies, leprosy, *kokumi* (a skin disease),
> incest of a man with his mother or daughter,
> with his mother-in-law or step-daughter, bes-
> tiality, calamities from creeping things, from
> the high gods, and from high birds, killing
> animals, bewitchments.[13]

Expiations for such offenses are to be made by
elaborate ritualized offerings, to which

"The Gods of Heaven, thrusting open the
adamantine door of Heaven and cleaving the
many-piled clouds of Heaven with an awful
waycleaving, ... (and) the gods of Earth,
climbing to the tops of the high mountains
and to the tops of the low mountains, sweep-
ing apart the mists of the high mountains and
the mists of the low mountains, *will lend
ear.*"[14]

Here are social ordinances given the dignity of
divine commands, the rude beginnings of a
moral consciousness destined to develop as we
shall see, with time and under the influence of
other religious ideas, into a full-blown ethical
system of which every item of genuinely social
adjustment is worthy of perpetuation in looking
forward to any more advanced moral and religious order.

Rather more significant than these crude
moral implications of a primitive faith, however, is the faith itself. And certainly here in
this secondary stage in the development of
Japan's religious consciousness the most significant aspect is a new, enlarged, and more vital
concept of deity than had previously commanded the imaginations and loyalties of men. That
their social ethics were limited by the animistic
and polytheistic assumptions of the day is easily
discernible. Japanese culture had gone as far
as it might without the introduction of certain
broadening and unifying agencies in thought,

and these Japan was destined to receive soon from her neighbors China and Korea, both far advanced at this time in culture and religion.

III. CHINESE CULTURE, INCLUDING
CONFUCIAN AND TAOIST ELEMENTS

The earliest evidence of Chinese influence in
Japan seems to point to contact between the two
countries as early as the first century B. C.
These earliest relationships may have been
purely commercial, perhaps even piratical, but
later there are indications of actual cultural ex-
changes.[1] In the heyday of *Han* and *Wei* culture in China one of the ideas we may suppose
to have been transmitted to Japanese shores was
a new emphasis upon the dual aspect of reality,
positive and negative. In the Nihongi (I.i),
whose Chinese ideology is well established, we
read: "Of old, Heaven and Earth were not separated and the *In* and the *Yo* (or *Yin* and
Yang, female and male principles, respectively)
were not yet divided." Perhaps it was this dual
concept which made possible the heightened
spiritualized appreciation of deity previously
mentioned. In any event, from an early date
we discover this dual conception of reality in
Japan, more or less corrected later by the Buddhist emphasis upon unity. This granted, what
we see in the existence of both concepts is a beginning of the interplay between the ideas of

transcendence and divine immanence, a happy alternation between which makes for richness of experience both earthly and supermundane.

Specifically we find the suggestion of dual relationship in life doing for Japan at this stage of history just what a similar concept has accomplished elsewhere in world history: it resulted in the deification and personification of all that seemed good and valuable, including the spirits of the departed loved ones, the heroic characters of the past, and even of certain living beings who were regarded as representatives or incarnations of the divine on earth, notably the emperors. Concerning this development Aston remarks, "In the case of the deification of living and dead Mikados there is much room for suspicion of foreign influence;"[2] and again, "China, always far ahead of Japan in spirituality, has exercised a profound influence on the development of Japanese ideas about spiritual matters."[3]

A. EMPEROR WORSHIP—"PRIESTHOOD OF SOVEREIGN."

It seems likely that one of the factors in the ready acceptance of Chinese culture at this time by the ruling authorities in Japan was the anticipation that there would result therefrom a definite stabilization of society.[4] The emperors were obviously having difficulty in reducing the native tribes throughout central Japan to sub-

mission and order. We see here a conscious
effort to enlist external and supernatural forces
in favor of stability. The result was the rise of
emperor worship, which has since been the very
core of Japanese political and religious philosophy. Whether this is a "blasphemous cult,"
as some regard it[5] is a debatable issue. We may
only here advance the possibility that, in consideration of the dignity and benevolence with
which the whole long line of rulers, with comparatively few exceptions, has borne this honor,
the exaltation of the emperor to the level of
deity, to whom all inhabitants of these as yet
uncivilized and disorganized islands should look
for supreme leadership, was and still remains
for millions of Japanese a potent reminder of
the supernatural in the natural realm. Surely
it was a forward step in the process of differentiating the natural from the eternal and then
of reuniting these spheres with a human link,
similar in character to the rationalized systems
of Christology which have sought to explain
Jesus' mediation between this world and its
Creator. The development of Mikado worship
in Japanese history may be regarded as a distinct landmark in the upward evolution of the
religious culture of the land. Particularly apt
is the idea of the "priesthood of the sovereign"
which Dr. Harada thinks a better interpretation
than "emperor-worship."[6]

B. ANCESTOR-WORSHIP AND DEIFICATION OF HEROES

Of like character and worthy of consideration under the same category of personalized deity is the worship of departed ancestors and of great heroes. It is a true urge which prompts men to identify those "loved long since and lost awhile" with the imperishable realm of the spirit. Belief in the persistence of something in our loved ones' natures beyond the grave exists in some form among all peoples and seems an inevitable corollary of the theorem, "Mankind is incurably religious." One Japanese apologist seeks to rationalize ancestor worship by asking, "How can we expect a man who feels no gratitude toward his own ancestors to have a true appreciation of the great mercy and goodness of God?"[7] Just as aptly may we ask, How can we expect a man who has no true appreciation of the great mercy and goodness of the Divine to feel that his ancestors, long since departed, mean anything in his life? These two concepts are inseparably bound up together. The dead, be they kindred or other worthy characters who once trod this mortal vale, are by the act of worship identified with the Ultimate which does not pass away and which, consciously or unconsciously, is regarded as the conserver of personal values and virtues.

All Japanese feel deeply the genuineness of the religious sanctions supporting ancestor worship and exaltation of the nation's heroic dead. Harada, a native son and a Christian, contends that "Reverence for the memory of the dead and tendance upon their spirits is not necessarily worship . . . . . The term 'communion of saints' comes nearer than worship to expressing the idea."[8]   Furthermore, there is close affinity to the traditional Christian sublimation of death as the crown of life when Japanese regard that commonly feared phenomenon as merely the deification to which the living may all look forward.   Dr. Nitobe properly evaluates this peculiarly Oriental custom and identifies it with the universal impulses of life: "I am far from identifying the Shinto with the Jewish faiths, but the idea of ancestor worship, if consistently practiced, will approach the Christian doctrine of immortality and the Jewish conception of monotheism."[9]   Here then is another religious value which, born of the spiritual needs of primitive Japan and cultivated by contact with Chinese thought, should not be lost sight of in any modern renaissance of religious culture.

C. TAOIST INFLUENCE — "MICHI", THE WAY OF THE GODS

Ancestor worship, deification of heroes, emperor worship, as practiced in Japan, all testify to a strong infiltration of Confucian thought. There are also evidences of the ingraftation of

Taoist ideas and principles.[10] Such influences may undoubtedly be seen in the expansion of the conception of *Michi* into what may today be regarded as "probably the most expressive term in the Japanese vocabulary of ethics and religion."[11] The Chinese equivalent is *Tao* which is the central idea in Taoism, "The Way, the Path, the Truth." Whether or not the Japanese evolved a regard for *Michi* prior to and independent of the Chinese equivalent is a moot point, one's conclusion depending upon his idea of the origins of the Japanese people. Perhaps we may resolve the divergent viewpoints by holding that whatever the most primitive conception of *Michi* may have been, it was unconscious of dependence upon the Chinese *Tao* until the relatively later period in which we are here treating it. In any event, by the time the term "Shinto" came to be used commonly to designate the "Higher Way" the Japanese had definitely filled the term with emphasis upon the divine origin of that Way : *Shin* meaning God or Gods, *to* the Japanese equivalent of *Tao,* and the complete expression *Shinto* denoting "The Way of the Gods."

Since that time Confucian and Taoist influences have been repeatedly brought to bear upon Shinto, even as they have reacted from the beginning in China,[12] and Japanese religion has inclined now to this, now to that point of view, as there has been emphasis in differing ages and atmospheres upon the ethical or upon the Ultimate. It is probable that Shinto was saved from the extremes of both Confucian intellectualism and Taoist fanaticism by the fact that the two systems were introduced into Japan as two aspects of the same "Way" and a harmonization developed peculiarly adapted to the Japanese temperament.

There is in most Christian quarters a willingness to recognize the ethical values of Confucianism; there should be equal readiness to see that Taoism, under the influence of Lao-tse, was seeking intuitively an Ultimate ground for such moral considerations. The two complemented each other in China and each was in turn deeply affected by the other, the social by the religious and the religious by the social. Perhaps the failure of either Confucianism or Taoism to adequately meet China's deepest needs resulted from unwillingness to let both ways of approach to life meet in one well-developed religious system. We see the benefits of such dual foci in Japanese religious thought following contact with both of these Chinese viewpoints and as later softened by Buddhist values, and these virtues should never be lost from the Japanese religious consciousness.

IV. BUDDHISM—THE MAHAYANA TYPE

Thus far we have noted three distinct stages in the development of the religious culture of Japan: the purely animistic, followed by a more or less spiritualized and personalized polytheism, and this in turn succeeded by the idealistic dualism corresponding to the prevailing mode of thought in the China of that day. Along with these developments the arts and social relationships of Japan likewise progressed until they reached a stage beyond which they could not advance until the scope and depth of the race's mental and spiritual life had been expanded by larger contact with the outside world and by the introduction of a religious philosophy more concerned with universals than anything yet known. These new factors were implicit in the introduction of Buddhism.

Buddhism came to Japan in the sixth century A.D. via Korea. The Korean ruling house in sending an image of Buddha and certain sacred books to the Japanese emperor seems to have been seeking an ally against the designs of an aggressive neighboring kingdom, and Japan seems to have deliberately accepted continental solutions to specific social and governmental

problems as the strongest bulwark against disaster whether from within or without.[1]   This
latter is evident in the avidity with which
Prince-Regent Shotoku seized upon the Confucian ideas which also accompanied Buddhist
teachings, and, writing these into a new consti-
tution, relied upon the Buddhist religion to en-
force the new provisions.[2]

Buddhism could not or did not attempt to
avoid this strange identification with Confucian
principles.   It is the genius of Buddhism to
affect such compromises in lands through which
it passes, even to the extent of losing its own
soul, in some opinions.[3] In particular, Buddhism
took over the five-fold relationships of the Confucian ethics.[4]   These will come in for further
consideration later under the head of Confucianism; suffice it here to say that this Confucian
ethic made possible for Buddhism that very ac-
commodating sliding scale of morality which
has been both its strength and its weakness in
Eastern Asia: the ascetic order at the one extreme for the holy man, a practical every-day
moral code for the man of affairs, and any inter-
mediate state desired for the somewhat pious.[5]

Nevertheless, Buddhism filled a long felt
need in Japanese life.   Its history is a fascinat-
ing story, but here we must be content to treat
only of those virtues and values which may be
fairly regarded as a permanent heritage in the

religious culture of Japan.

A. UNIVERSALISM — A BROADER PHILOSOPHY — A KIND OF ABSOLUTE

First let us glimpse that broad view of reality and of life itself which Buddhism presents wherever there is any loyalty whatsoever to the ideas of its founder. Many prefer to call it the universal outlook; perhaps it would be better styled Pantheism. Yet even for the pantheist there is a unity — a kind of Absolute as wide as the universe and as powerful. Dr. W. Gundert, in speaking of the Sanron sect which was the first type of Buddhism to be taught in Japan, remarks that it "had for the Japanese the merit of ensuring the mystical character of the Absolute, and to point out its essential identity with empiric existence."[6] Dr. A. K. Reischauer comments, "It is the very breath of the philosophy of Mahayana Buddhism to reduce the plurality of being to an all-embracing Divine Whole, and to regard the myriad of gods and individual beings as in some way the expression of the All-One."[7] And again, "The higher side of Buddhism has always stood for the conception of a universe of rational laws which man must obey if he would advance to a larger and nobler life."[8]

Here we have the groundwork of a lofty philosophy of life and for an enlarging conception of man's destiny. The permanent value of such a universalized view of reality can scarcely be doubted, since Christianity stresses a similar unity in its own rationalizations. The relation of this Buddhist philosophy to man's destiny, as it unfolded in Japanese history, introduces us to the peculiar subjectivity of that with which Buddhism concerns itself, and to this we must give a moment's consideration.

B. SUBJECTIVE VIEW OF LIFE — CONDITION OF INNER PEACE

Buddhism frankly admits that its universe, insofar as it may be known at all, is a subjective reality. This is inevitable in the Buddhist way of approaching and seeking to escape the misery of existence. Gundert comments on how, in reducing all to a unity "by a process of analytical dissolution of all concepts which, to the ordinary man, constitute his universe," the Buddhist thinker is confronted by a subjective reality "not as a universe including man, but as man including the universe of his experience."[9] Also "Buddhists are realists (i.e. not agnostics or nihilists) in the sense that they recognize a reality, but an absolute reality, which is beyond or behind the empirical world and its whirl-like movements, a reality which is indiscernable, inexpressible, and without any movement, a reality the attainment of which means perfect salvation."[10]

This subjectivity of Buddhism's approach to life, if understood, gives the key to many of the otherwise opaque aspects of Oriental religion and culture.   Prepared to see eye to eye with an Oriental is not to be disturbed by large un-rationalized areas of objective reference, pro-vided the heart is right and all is calm within. Thus *Nirvana* takes on far more meaning than were possible to the Occidental who insists upon conceiving it in Space, Time, or some other di-mension of objectivity.[11]   There is something here for the Christian to cogitate in seeking to evaluate the mores of the inscrutable East; for, while we believe Jesus' words had distinct ob-jective reference also when he said, "The King-dom of God is within you," he was obviously doing his best to bring it closer than some "far off divine event."   He was striving to make it an experiential kingdom of peace and harmon-ization, our inner selves with that reality with-out to which our experiences bear testimony. The Oriental religions have much to contribute to this same peace of mind for which we all crave, and here is one valuable element in Bud-dhism's contribution to the religious culture of Japan which no critique should overlook as an aid in that realization.

C. SELF-REALIZATION THROUGH INTROSPECTION

Another aspect of this subjectivity of reference much emphasized in the Buddhist system is that imperative urge to self-realization through introspection which constantly stimulates the devout Buddhist to bring his life and his environment into conformity with the highest ideals known. After extensive travelling in Japan, a prominent American scientist, the late Dr. Elmer E. Sperry, gave it as his opinion within the writer's hearing that this habit of self-realization through introspection, i.e. comparison of one's state each day with the ideal sought — has been the chief factor in Japan's remarkable progress in the past fifty years.

This attitude helps to explain the willingness of this ancient and tradition-bound people to cast off that which is obsolete as soon as something better is available, and it also casts some light on their peculiarly Oriental tendency to adapt each new idea or tool to fit the facts of life as seen by the Japanese themselves. Progress in Buddhist lands has been in full face of all the stern aspects of existence, be they however evil. This becomes apparent as we think of the remarkable pluck and determination shown by the Japanese in reconstructing the present and beautiful city of Tokyo on the very funeral pyres of a hundred-thousand stricken loved ones; and that with full knowledge that a similar disaster may occur again at any moment. However the new buildings are of concrete and steel, the streets are wide and straight as protection against future fires, and new sanitary provisions will in a very few years save as many lives as were snuffed out in the 1923 disaster—and yet Tokyo is essentially Japanese.

Such accomplishments would never have been possible among the easy-going nature worshippers with whom we were dealing earlier in this paper. Certain harsh and stern realities had been employed effectively to prod the Japanese wide awake. It was Buddhism by which "these people who had long ceased to be naive children of nature were led to the conscious consideration of the problem of life, and to self-introspection."[12] There are no finer teachings concerning self-examination than certain verses in the Buddhist scriptures: "The Boddhisattva knows nothing but his own heart. And why is this? Because he who knows his own heart knows the heart of all beings, and he whose heart is pure, to him the heart of every being is pure."[13a] And again, "First examine yourself and then others; first examine your own will and then the will of others; first examine your own principles and then the principles of others."[13b] Has Christianity produced any finer subjective fruits than the finest of Buddhist products? The Christian cause can never be assured of ultimate success in Japan until, in addition to its characteristic social passion, it shall also be seen to develop the conditions of inner peace through introspection and self-mastery which have been the noblest fruits of Buddhist piety throughout the centuries.

D. RESTRAINT AND RESIGNATION — SUBMISSION TO KARMA

Closely allied with this principle of introspection is that other typically Buddhist quality which for lack of simpler phraseology we may style self-restraint and resignation to the inevitability of *Karma*. While doubtless this gospel has imparted to lands predominantly Buddhist a somewhat negative and pessimistic attitude toward life, it has nonetheless, as Harada contends, "worked powerfully for Japanese culture and refinement, . . . counter-balancing the frivolous tendencies of the time" in the Nara and Heian eras.[14] The Japanese were by nature originally a cheerful, optimistic and fairly emotional people, if we may judge from the earliest literature extant. Buddhism brought to Nippon a more serious attitude. It taught the impermanence of all things, except the certainty "Be sure your Karma will find you out."[15] Cause-and-effect is for the Buddhist the supreme law of existence. Every deed has its consequence; every thought as well. Misdeeds bring only future sorrow. This is the surest thing in the Buddhist teaching. The only escape from worse misery is to restain one's self from committing evil in thought or deed, and thus avoid starting the inexorable train of cause and effect. Once deeds or misdeeds are committed there is no way of circumventing their issue. Effect follows cause as the night the day, and more certainly,—the one changeless reality in a changing world.

Full comprehension of this supreme law and resignation to it is Enlightenment, both spiritual and moral. The enlightened practice restraint from the known sins, and then are reconciled to the conditions of life over which they have no power. Thus are they relieved of worry about results and outcomes which they cannot avoid. It is like following the Pauline injunction, "Be not conformed to this world," and being sure also "in whatsoever state . . . . to be content."[16] In this there is genuine virtue, if not carried too far. It explains the "shi-kata-ga nai" (can't be helped) attitude of the Japanese in their great disasters; it helps them to forget the past, and inspires them not to be unduly alarmed for the future. It approximates trust in the orderliness of Providence in Christian circles, and is but another important unit in the ever-rising edifice of Japanese religious consciousness.

The way is now prepared for the consideration of two other Buddhist virtues which have
their roots in this unchangeable law of Karma.
They are the ideas of Justice and Mercy.

E. THE IDEA OF JUSTICE — IMPLIED MORAL RESPONSIBILITY

The inevitability of effect following cause
suggests a rough justice in the universe. It is
a Buddhist postulate. And since punishment of
misdeeds is inexorable in the cosmic realm it
should be so likewise in any social order. Upon
this rock is erected the Buddhist moral code, of
which Professor Anesaki says, "Buddhist ethics
is so anxious to prevent the arising of bad
thoughts and actions that it surpasses almost all
other ethical systems in enumerating human
weaknesses and vices."[17]

Such a concept of moralized justice man to
man, and man toward the Cosmos, would of
necessity eventually seek its logical conclusion
in a claim for justice from that Cosmos in recognition of lives of introspection, resignation
and restraint. That demand was forthcoming
not many generations after Buddhism gained
foothold in Japan. Dr. Anesaki comments, "In
the midst of solemn ceremonies and the luxu-
rious splendour of life, the evanescence of
worldly things was felt and the aspiration for
an eternal bliss became conspicuous."[18] We can-

not follow this thought further here without impinging upon a sphere of future discussion, but now let it be only observed that in the concept of social justice rooted in universal justice we have a religious value of noblest magnitude.

F. MERCY — TO ALL LIFE — A COSMIC ATTRIBUTE

But the human heart is never content with mere justice, either for itself or for others. This is most evident in the philosophy of Mahayana, and receives utmost emphasis in Japanese Buddhism. If it seems out of harmony with genuine and original Buddhism, it is because we have discovered just one more regard in which Northern Buddhism outgrew its founder's faith. If the Cosmos is just, it must also be merciful. Justice alone is not a sufficiently broad and firm foundation for the relations of a home, nor of a social group; how can it be adequate for the needs of the universe? The prophetic utterance of Micah (6.8) was from the very heart of the human race in its convictions about the heart of Reality: Justice, Mercy and all that should inspire in man humility and devotion must find its home in and back of the Universe itself.

All authorities agree that one of Buddhism's greatest contributions to Japanese culture lay in the inculcation of the "virtues of gentleness, pity and sympathy."[19] Concerning the emergence of these virtues Dr. Reischauer says, "It is not strange that this is so, for especially the virtues of pity and sympathy for others grow directly out of the Buddhist view as to the nature of human life. Life is suffering, and sympathy becomes a natural attitude of mind and heart."[20] But Mercy with the Japanese Buddhist, wherever it may have had its origin, is something more ultimate than mere mutual sympathy man to man. Mercy has been definitely imputed by Mahayana Buddhism to that which is behind the natural realm; to wit, the many handed goddess of Mercy, *Kwannon*, whose ubiquitous images represent the most popular of Japanese deities and who is identified with the Eternal Buddha in the *Tendai* and *Jodo* sects. Further evidence that mercy and sympathy are inherent in the universal order is also found in the inclusion of all beings, even birds and plants, in the scope of man's moral obligation of sympathy and spiritual communion.[21] There is a deep bond of fellowship between the Buddhists and Christianity's Little-Brother-of-the-Birds-and-Flowers, St. Francis; for no good disciple of Gautama Buddha would willfully injure one of the least of these, since they are fellow-creatures in a suffering world.

Even more significant has been the influence of the spirit of sympathy and mercy in Japanese social relationships. Here there is ample proof of the superiority of the Buddhist moral ideals over those by which Japan had lived prior to the coming of "Enlightenment." We read that Prince Shotoku had no sooner become a devout believer in the Buddha-Way than he began the reorganization of his government, in the course of which he established four departments of benevolence and mercy: (1) an educational department, (2) a dispensary, (3) a hospital for malignant diseases, and (4) an asylum for the dependent aged and orphans.[22]

To a marked degree this merciful spirit continues to this day to motivate the Japanese people. Visitors to the island empire marvel at that phenomenal social solidarity which, so long as any have food, will permit none of the family to starve or go unclothed, be they but distant cousins. This explains why even in times of economic depression and distress there is comparatively little of destitution and starvation, and far less of reported unemployment than in other civilized countries. There is in this, of course, a large element of the family loyalty of Shinto and of Confucian benevolence, but when one sees beggars going from door to door soliciting rice or small coins in Buddha's name, and seldom being refused at least a mite, it must be concluded that mercy has found permanent abiding place in the heart of Buddhist Japan.

G. HARMONY OF DEMOCRACY AND CULTURE

Justice and mercy in Buddhist lands doubtless spring in part from the assumption that
"any being might once have been our relation:
father, mother, brother, sister."[23] But there is a
deeper source than this. Buddhism is essentially
democratic. Gautama Buddha was an enemy of
the caste system and of all other artificial social
gradations in India. And, as Harada admirably
expresses it, "If Buddhism were allowed to
come to its logical conclusion, it would force
one to regard everything and all things as on an
equal footing. Neither money, rank, honor, nor
any other thing in the world can differentiate
one man from another. Even racial and national
differences are not to be regarded . . . . . The
universe is one; wealth and poverty are constantly changing; both snow and ice become the
water of the same brook. In truth a brotherhood having boundless possibilities has foundations here laid, upon which may be built an
enduring social structure through Great Enlightenment."[24]

To many, Democracy and Culture seem mu-
tually exclusive. Buddhism seems to have
bridged the chasm, to some degree at least, in
Japan. It is worthy of note that within a century or two after the Buddhist missionaries arrived, bringing the art and culture of both
China and Korea, there were produced in Japan

certain masterprieces of the fine arts of which
one scholar can say, "If one would see the highest development of Asiatic art, one has to turn
to Japan for specimens."[25] Prior to the dawn-
ing of her modern era Japan experienced three
great cultural advances, corresponding to the
rise of three distinct schools of Buddhist
thought and identified with the Nara, Heian
and Kamakura ages in the empire's political
history. During these centuries Japan's finest
emotional and intellectual sentiments found expression in sculpture, architecture, painting,
music, and, even more particularly "in literature, as is evidenced not by moral and religious
writings alone or chiefly, but by poems, novels,
dramas, and operatic libretto, as in the classical
No dances."[26]

The development of culture among a people,
however, depends largely upon freedom and
opportunity for self-expression. The arts flour-
ished in times when there was little or no religious or political oppression in Japan; they de-
clined when the social institutions became corrupt and tyrannical. Although Buddhism is in
essence universal and democratic, it has never
seemed able to perpetuate such traditions
among the upper-classes. Japan today is aristocratic to a high degree. Yet the ready willingness of the Japanese to recognize and ac-
claim any man whose talents or achievements

are of value to the social order—even to make a commoner Premier, and to exalt a son of the slums to sainthood—indicates that the inter-relationship between democracy and culture has not been entirely forgotten. Buddhism has had large part in cultivating that high degree of refinement which one finds even among the lowly in Japan. It must never be lost.

H. THE BEGINNINGS OF NON-RESISTANCE AND INTERNATIONALISM

The writer cannot refrain here from pursuing the logic of Buddhism and the facts of Japanese history to the conclusion that cultural progress, such as the Japanese had already achieved in an age when our Anglo-Saxon and Teutonic forefathers were still barbarians, is inevitably identified with a broad and all-inclusive humanitarian philosophy. We have seen that Buddhist mercy and justice have led many in Asiatic lands to visions of universal brotherhood. It is true that, for the most part, these have been only visions and logical deductions, but in Japan's early relationships with Korea, China, India and other lands we see a growing tendency to transcend social, national and even racial lines in order to secure and to exchange those things which make for mutual advancement.

Throughout the long history of Asia, though

many of its pages are stained with blood, Buddhism's influence has been largely cast on the side of peace, good-will, cultural exchange and adaptation. Prince Shotoku, in conversion to Buddhism, was also converted to Buddhism's gospel of identity with all other life. Dr. Anesaki has shown how this seventh century ruler became an apostle of non-resistance in all but his attitude toward evil, and how his children pursued the same policy even when all that Shotoku had sought to establish seemed to require defense from its enemies.[27]

It would be utter folly, in the light of Japan's feudalistic history and more recent martial imperialism, to try to make out a case for the Japanese today as disciples of Shotoku in such peaceful pursuits. Japan as a nation is no less nationalistic, imperialistic, militaristic than her Occidental neighbors, and as this is being written she appears to some even more open to criticism on these scores. Yet, facing their own people Japanese militarists have had to use some word other than "war" to designate what has been happening recently in Manchuria and elsewhere in China. "Self-defense" propaganda has been used not only to placate foreign opinion but for home-consumption as well. And just as in the West the slogan "The war to end war" was used shamelessly to ensnare military support from a peace-loving public from 1914 to

1918, so in Japan now it is "for the sake of the peace of the Far East" that the public is urged to give lavishly of life-blood and of money to the imperial armies and navies.

Yet ever and anon some incident arises to demonstrate that the Buddhist and Oriental principle of "harmlessness" has not left itself without witnesses even among the Japanese. Perhaps the most outstanding recent demonstration was the prevailing sentiment in Japan following the enactment by the American Congress of the 1924 "Exclusion" legislation. Early reactions in Tokyo and other cities, as the writer well remembers, were violent and many hot-bloods were for prompt and forceful dramatization of the "grave consequences" prophesied in Washington as the probable outcome of such legislation. But wiser counsel soon prevailed, and the Japanese thereupon reconciled themselves to the longer processes of time and good-will which they hope will convince the United States of the wrongness of such discrimination. In this Japan was essentially Asiatic and Buddhist. It is unfortunate that she does not always follow such peaceful tactics, but prefers to act toward China as the "Christian" nations have traditionally done. Yet we have discovered in Japan's Buddhist background the beginnings of the spirit of inter-cultural, international, inter-racial fair-play which, in spite of occasional interruptions, will eventually bring the Japanese into full cooperation with the rest of the world-family and into complete accord with the principle of non-resistance which is a part of their Buddhist heritage.

I. THE ETERNAL BUDDHA — AN APPROACH TO THEISM

In all of these regards, however, which involve a world-affirming philosophy and a hope of transforming society along ideal lines, it must be constantly borne in mind that Japanese Buddhism takes an attitude very different from the original convictions of Gautama regarding the universe and human life. Before reaching Japan, even before leaving India, Buddhism had undergone profound changes. In passing through China and Korea other great alterations were made in conformity with the beliefs and habits of the peoples encountered. The type of Buddhism first to reach Japan was what is sometimes known as Provisional Mahayana.[28] It soon became apparent that even such a modified form of the Indian religion was not so well adapted to the situation in Japan as certain other types which were farther emancipated from the original Buddhist, or Hinayana, tradition. The Buddhism which eventually captured Japan was an extreme form of Mahayana known as Tendai, the central principles of which, together with the scripture *Saddharma*

Pundarika,[29] were brought from China by a visiting Japanese priest known now as *Dengyo Daishi* at the close of the eighth century. Dengyo Daishi had an equally illustrious disciple, known today as *Kobo Daishi*[30] who also had studied in China. When his master Dengyo was dead Kobo Daishi began to preach the full implications of the Tendai doctrine of the "Eternal Buddha," which corresponds far more closely to the Absolute of positive religion than anything Gautama Buddha ever postulated.

Of such an all-inclusive character was the Eternal One that all the known deities of Japan or other lands could be embraced therein. Accordingly, Kobo Daishi contended that in essence Amaterasu, the Sun Goddess, was but an incarnation in the early history of Japan of the Indian god *Vairochana*, and that all the other native deities corresponded to certain of the aspects of reality which Buddhism had also distinguished as gods of this world. There began also with Kobo Daishi that movement of coalescence between Buddhism and the native cult of Japan which came to be known as *Ryobu-Shinto* (The Two-fold Way of the Gods). Of this we shall speak a little later, but what we must here observe is that Japanese religion had caught a vision of one great, all-inclusive Reality in which all things live and move and have their beings; a pantheistic conception with polytheistic fringes, yet so tinged with purposeful idealism as to give it much of the character of monotheism. For, as Reischauer points out, Kobo Daishi was preaching that "man can even in this present life attain Buddhahood, since he is a essentially one with the Eternal."[31] This is somewhat akin to Jesus' thought of himself as "in the Father, and the Father in him," and to his injunction to his disciples to be like-minded, "Be ye therefore perfect even as your heavenly Father is perfect."[32]

J. IDEALISTIC REALISM — PSEUDO-SCIENTIFIC CONTROL OF CIRCUMSTANCES FOR MAN'S GOOD BY THE "TRUE WORD" FORMULA

With this new identification of all the sacred history of Japan with the Eternal Buddha came a fresh sense of the oneness of all things and the rise of a system of thought which has much in common with that of Idealistic-realism, and even in some regards with Humanism today. If the Eternal Buddha embraced all, argued Kobo Daishi, then most assuredly all things were sacred; there was no dividing line between the divine and the sacred.[33] It was his conviction also that the Eternal Buddha was in reality merely a "world of ideas" of which there might be many counterparts in the phenomenal realm. On this reasoning Kobo established a new religious order known as the Shingon sect. *Shin*=

True, *gon* = word, and it was his contention
that if we but have the proper attitude in the
use of ordered symbols and rituals—i.e. the
"True Word" — we may lay hold upon the
source of things, "the world of ideas," and
thereby control the phenomenal aspects of existence.[34] A form of magic this was, to be sure,
but—like Alchemy—so rationalized as to appear inescapable, a primitive pseudo-science.

Truth there was in it, however, and power;
as is evidenced by Kobo Daishi's versatile life
and accomplishments. He is hailed today as the
originator of silk-worm culture, has a reputa-
tion in sculpture, was the inventor of the Japanese syllabary by which all can read and write
simple Japanese, and is regarded as the father
of popular education. Whatever we may think
of his metaphysics, this man had laid hold upon
certain deep truths (shin-gon) which made ac-
cessible for him and for his country many blessings until then unknown in Japan. We of the
West are today seeking the magic formula for
unlocking the treasure houses of true happiness
and lasting prosperity. Even our best in science
is not infallible, however, and we shall do well
not to ignore this "true-word" key to the Eternal in its fullest implications concerning the
values of life.

K. "SALVATION — BY FAITH" IN AMIDA — SAVED FROM TRANSMIGRATION TO THE "PURE LAND" — BODDHISATTVA-HOOD, SALVATION FOR SERVICE

Japanese Buddhism was evolving, and the end of the process was not yet. The implications of Justice, of Mercy, and of Eternal Oneness are far-reaching. Implicit in the Mahayana gospel is a ray of hope for humanity which otherwise is trapped in this vale of tears with no chance of escape. From the earliest days of the disagreement of Mahayanists with Hinayanists in India there was mention of a saving principle which even antedated Gautama, and which is by many Buddhists worshipped as akin to the Supreme, *Amitabha* (Infinite Light) or Amitayus (Infinite Life).[35] Worshipped as the Eternal, this *Amida* (pronounced thus, or *Amita*, in Japanese) promises to the faithful a place in his Western Paradise of the "Pure Land" beyond the grave. Many believe Amida to have had at least one incarnation on earth, but that the *Hozo Bosatsu* who is widely thought of as that incarnated "Saviour" was not a historical character, so far as any record discloses, disturbs none who in faith utter the "*Namu Amida Butsu*" (I adore thee, Boundless Buddha. They worship no earthly creature, but look to a heavenly city not made with hands.

In Japanese Buddhism this idea of divine salvation has been developed into a doctrine approximating the Christian faith in the saving grace of Christ;[36] for with the great *Honen* (1133-1212) and *Shinran* (1173-1262), founders in the late Heian era of the *Jodo* (Pure Land) and the *Shin* (True) sects, one has but to take the formula "Namu Amida Butsu" in faith upon his lips to be assured of hope and ultimate salvation.[37] There are many, of course, who feel that this salvation is a very different conception from that held by Christianity.[38] Dr. Harada, for example, contends that "It is deliverance from the miserable world, or in other words, escape from the miserable stages of transmigration."[39] It is true, there is certain divergence from the Christian idea in this and other regards, but as between the Mahayanist acceptance of a dualism of Buddha-realm vs. this sphere of misery and suffering, and that very marked dualism of Paul and the early eschatologically inclined Christians—earth vs. heaven, flesh vs. spirit—there seems no great difference in kind.

If we turn then to that idea of the Kingdom of God as beginning here and now for all who realize that the Kingdom is not only something subjective but "within" seeking objective expression, there is also the Mahayanist counterpart in the notion of Boddhisattva-hood to which the good Buddhist aspires in thoughts and deeds in the present life, and which, having attained the blessed state, he promptly renounces as a happy reward that he may return to earth to serve and save his fellow-men.[40] That this is a beautiful spirit and a noble ideal none will deny. It compares favorably with the Christian view of salvation for service. It is the writer's conviction that the superiority of the Christian trust in, and power to realize, salvation consists not in the nature of the ideal itself but in the background of a different supporting religious philosophy and history. The spirit of hope and of ultimate salvation, and especially this doctrine of salvation for service, to be found in Mahayana Buddhism today are clearly ingraftations upon a religious philosophy and tradition basically and originally pessimistic, unsocial, self-centered, and without any such hope of ultimate personal triumph. This, it seems assured, in large measure accounts for the wide disparity between the ideal in Japanese Buddhism and the actual rather low level of moral achievement in the lives of its adherents. Other factors, such as the persistence of many as yet unmoralized primitive mores, must be taken into account, to be sure; but if, as Reischauer believes, "It must be admitted. . . . .that Buddhism in the lives of the great majority of its adherents is often a real hindrance to the higher life,"[41] it is due largely to these historic factors, and not to the ideal of salvation which the most aggressive Buddhists are today preaching. Regardless of its source the bifocal idea of salvation—of self, and for service—is a value of highest spiritual and moral significance for the future of Japanese life.

L. BUDDHISM'S MORALIZING EFFECT UPON EARLIER MORES.

Christian missionaries find these already well-developed moral and spiritual concepts a distinct advantage in the work of inculcating Christian ideals and beliefs. If the results in the infiltration of Japanese society with Christian principles have seemed more gratifying than in some other lands, it is doubtless because of the already highly advanced state of religious culture found there by the missionaries on arrival.

All this was largely the work of Buddhism which, in addition to inculcating the lofty principles herein designated, did much to give a moral emphasis to the customs which it found in Japan and could not or did not care to supplant. The previously mentioned values in the primitive mores of Japan—the spirit of awe and reverence, with a desire for worship, prayer and communion, in the presence of superhuman agencies; the later developed sense of kinship, gratitude and love toward the somewhat personalized and spiritualized *Kami*; the feeling of individual responsibility imposed thereby, expressing itself in attention to formal purity and a primitive code of morals; the exaltation of the imperial rulers to divinity as earthly representatives of the gods; the elevation of deceased loved ones and great heroes to the sublimity of deity and the hope of themselves passing into such a "communion"; the idea of *Michi*, the Way, by which the highest and best in life is attained,—all of these early concepts were by Buddhism in some degree moralized and ennobled through more than a millennium of intimate contact and inter-mixture.[42] The story of this complex process of integration with the primitive faith, together with the assimilation and partial moralization of much therein, is one that has never yet been adequately explored. We may only in the following chapter mention certain permanent values that came out of this fusion and have left their mark in the religious consciousness of the Japanese nation.

V. RYOBU-SHINTO—MERGING OF BUD-
DHISM WITH SHINTO

We have thus far intentionally refrained
from the extensive use of the term "Shinto" to
designate the native religion of Japan. This is
because we are assured that "Shinto as a term
came into general use as a result of the
heightening of national consciousness during
the early period of the struggle with Buddhism
as a foreign faith."[1] It is significant that Shinto
is not referred to by this name in either the Kojiki or the Nihongi. Perhaps the Buddhists
themselves coined the term to help along the
identification with the native faith sought by
Kobo Daishi and his colleagues. The merged
Buddhist and native faiths were to be regarded
as the "Two-fold Way of the Gods," i.e. *Ryobu-
Shinto,* a term used freely throughout the millennium of merged identity. The extent to
which this was a genuine merger of the two
faiths is indicated by Dr. D. C. Holtom in his
"Study of the Political Philosophy of Shinto" as
follows: "By the opening of the ninth century
the doctrinal assimilation of Buddhism and
Shinto had been accomplished, so that now
Buddhist rites were conducted at Shinto shrines,

while priests prayed to Shinto gods under Buddhist names."[2]   Most Christian scholars feel that the union—"compromise" Dr. Reischauer calls it—was a disaster and a blunder. Perhaps it was for institutional Buddhism, but for Japan its practical benefits at least challenge the complacency of the "total loss" viewpoint.

A. POPULARIZATION OF A SENSE OF THE UNITY AND SERIOUSNESS OF LIFE

One of the significant results of this Buddhist-Shinto merger was the popularization of the Buddhist view of the oneness and seriousness of all life. It is doubtful if in any other way the enlargement of Buddhism's sphere of influence in Japan could have been so effectively accomplished. As to method, the incident compares to the credit of Buddhism, with that form of compromise affected by Constantine in introducing Christianity officially to Europe, and one should certainly prefer this Buddhist means of indoctrination to those coercive measures employed in Christ's name for the evangelization of Northern Europe. That the Buddhist indoctrination of Japan was complete, or nearly so, is attested by all; Buddhism is yet "the religion of the great bulk of the Japanese people."[3] When Shinto and Buddhism were officially separated in 1870, the masses were not disturbed in their dual faith, but largely remained both

Shintoists and Buddhists; Shintoists in politics and on festal occasions, Buddhists in the serious affairs of life and death.[4]

B. DEVELOPMENT OF THE SPIRIT OF TOLERANCE

One other effect of this religious merger in Japanese life should be noted in passing, viz. the creation of a spirit of tolerance in religious and intellectual matters. Buddhism, especially the Mahayana, has usually been tolerant toward other faiths. We find evidence of this in the accretions to Buddhism from practically every other religion with which it has had contact. This was certainly true in the relationships with Shinto, and today, as we shall see a little later, the same can be said concerning Buddhism's contacts with Christianity. The religion of Enlightenment has shown itself willing to give and take wherever distinct advantage to itself as a religion might result. It is not unusual for Buddhists to open their temple grounds, even their monasteries, for Christian gatherings and conferences. Christian speakers are sometimes invited to Buddhist meetings. This spirit has in turn communicated itself to the Japanese people as a whole. The tolerant attitude of the Japanese toward differing religious and cultural viewpoints finds frequent expression in the literature of the empire, and nowhere better than in the well-known verse of a popular bard:

"By routes diverse men may the mountain
        climb,
    Each path presenting different views, sub-
        lime,—
But when to the proud summit they do rise,
    The self-same smiling moon doth greet all
        eyes."[5]

To be sure, there are dangers that tolerance
shall degenerate into indifference toward the
highest values of life, concerning which religions are considerably at variance. But there
is also large virtue in the Psalmist's exclama-
tion, "Behold how good and pleasant it is for
brethren to dwell together in unity,"[6] a satisfaction which many non-Christian Japanese understand more fully than some Christians. Ryobu-
Shinto had large share in this development of a
serious spirit of unity and tolerance, but the popular philosophy of the day was a highly superstitious brand of Monism, more significant for
the future development of Japanese religious
thought along universal lines than for any more
positive cultural values to be considered as the
outgrowth thereof. Confucian thought also
played considerable part in this evolution, and
must be studied in close association with the
Ryobu-Shinto epoch.

VI. CONFUCIANISM—AS A MORAL PHILOSOPHY

Let us now turn attention to the influence of the moral philosophy of Confucianism in Japan. Dr. W. E. Griffis is undoubtedly right in asserting that "the time when Chinese learning entered Japan by way of Korea has not been precisely ascertained. It is possible that letters and writings were known in some parts of the country as early as the fourth century, but it is nearly certain that, outside the Court of the Emperor, there was scarcely even a sporadic knowledge of the literature of China until the Korean missionaries of Buddhism had obtained a lodgment in the Mikado's capital."[1]

We must not assume, however, that Japan's first introduction to Chinese morality was by way of Korea. It is possible—indeed, probable —that the racial relationship of the Japanese with the Chinese is far closer and more diréct than this. If, as Brinkley affirms, one of the strains of blood entering into the Japanese composite was pure Chinese,[2] it would have been natural that certain Chinese mores should have been introduced from the first into the Japanese social structure. We may also be certain of more or less merchantile and diplomatic contact between the islands and the mainland from the earliest years of the Christian era.[3]   We have knowledge of the importation of a Chinese scholar near the end of the fourth century to teach at the Japanese court, and we know that certain emperors and princes were enamored of and versed in Confucian principles in the fifth and sixth centuries.[4]

With the arrival of Buddhist missionaries, both Korean and Chinese, moreover, the floodgates were opened for a deluge of Chinese influence.   And very soon thereafter Japan began to send her own scholars to China to study at the sources of culture and refinement.   The Buddhists, as previously mentioned, preached a gospel of spiritual enlightenment which was inextricably associated with continental civilization, very much as Occidental missionaries have confused European civilization with Christianity in more recent times.   Whatever the factors involved, we may accept Prof. Knox's contention that "long before 712 A.D. Confucian ethics had come to control conduct."[5] This is the date of the publication of the Kojiki which, even though the author thereof seems anxious to produce a truly Japanese document, shows large evidence of Chinese influence. Eight years later (720), as we have seen, appeared the Nihongi, in which the Kojiki's author collaborated in

producing what is in many respects more truly
a piece of Chinese than of Japanese literature.
Therein we are led to believe that, although the
acceptance of Confucian philosophy was a later
development, Japanese society submitted to the
dictates of Confucian ethics even before being
thoroughly indoctrinated with Buddhist concepts, an important fact to be kept in mind in
any survey of later history.

A. THE SACREDNESS OF THE FAMILY — SECRET OF SOCIAL SOLIDARITY

Undoubtedly the most elemental of the Chinese social principles adopted by Japan was the
sacredness of the family, patriarchally conceived.   In more primitive times the people of
Japan, insofar as they had any family loyalties,
followed the matriarchal principle.[6]   In some
ways the order resembled the freedom of con-
tract, man with woman, common in the Western
world today, although the monogamous relation
with its peculiar system of loyalties was quite
unknown.[7]   True order and regularity in family
life were not achieved until the acceptance of
the Chinese ideal.[8] Thereafter we find a rapidly
developing moral conscience on marital and filial relations, which made loyalty to the family
the most sacred of social obligations in Japan as
in China.

We cannot here enter any comparative dis-

cussion of the merits of the Oriental family
system as over against our Western recognition
of the freedom of youth in social relationships
and in choosing their own life-mates, the separ-
ation of young married couples from parents in
home-building, the proper relationships of children in the home, etc. Nevertheless, it is significant that the Chinese system has endured
through the centuries and still holds Asiatic
society steady, whereas the introduction of
Western individualism in Oriental family circles
has, for the most part, resulted in disorder and
disintegration. There are many good reasons
for believing this secret of social solidarity in
Oriental society in the past worthy of being re-
tained in preference to the introduction of modern foreign standards which are inseparably
bound up with Western traditions and institutions. Doubtless the Japanese women, as well
as the fathers and their children, must make
adaptations to meet many new and vexing social
problems in the decades immediately ahead;
the family loyalties a hundred years from now
will probably be quite different from those we
now observe; but in the main it would seem that
the family unit as developed in China, adopted
by Japan and Korea, and corresponding in general with the systems in force among most Oriental peoples, notably the Jews, is best adapted
to the needs of the East, and is perhaps in some

respects worthy of emulation by the extremely
individualistic West.   Hence the sacredness of
the family is here given as the sine-qua-non of
regular and healthy social life in the Orient,
and designated as a highly valuable element in
the religious culture of Japan.   It came as one
of the offerings of Confucianism.

B. THE FIVE RELATIONS — LOYALTY, FILIAL PIETY, CONJUGALITY, PRIMOGENITURE, FIDELITY

Having seen the Chinese family idea introduced within Japan we are obliged to refer to
the religious and moral sanctions which gave
the conception impetus and power.   In China
these were the Confucius-Mencius and Taoist
religious traditions previously mentioned.   Yet
none of these, as such,'were widely comprehended in Japan in these early centuries.   Rather, as
we have seen, Buddhism furnished the vehicle by
which the Confucian moral code was seriously
imposed upon Japan.   For Buddhism, in its so-
journ through India, Parthia, Scythia, China and
Korea, and thence to Japan, found that an ethic
of detachment from the entangling web of an
evil world was suited only for monks and other
unsocial creatures and that for successful prop-
agation of the Buddhist faith another code of
social principles would have to be found which
would apply with fairly good results among the
practically minded masses.[9]   Such a practical

code of ethics was found in the Confucian Five
Relations of Propriety, and in its further progress eastward Buddhism employed these principles as its own.

These five relations are:[10] (i) Service of one's
father, i.e. filial piety; (ii) Service of one's
prince or ruler, i.e. patriotic loyalty; (iii) Propriety between husband and wife, i.e. conju-
gality; (iv) Subordination of the younger to the
older offspring, i.e. primogeniture, with all its
implications; (v) Regard for friends, i.e. fidelity.[11] This system the Japanese took over in-
tact, with one emendation: whereas the Chinese
put first in all social relationships regard for
father, the Japanese, perhaps inspired from imperial sources, put first service of one's prince,
or loyalty, which is second in the Chinese order.
A perfectly logical alteration it was, too, in a
land engaged in building a strong consciousness
of national solidarity with the monarch as head
and father of a great mass of as yet incomplete-
ly assimilated subject-children.

This is the beginning in the development of
that all-encompassing patriotism which unites
the Japanese in utter loyalty to the will of their
emperor, and at the same times puts such great
stress on the importance of filial piety and of
fidelity to all one's relatives, neighbors and the
community.[12] For anyone who knows the Japanese nation well there can be no doubt of the

moral power of these Confucian ideals in moulding the lives of its people, from the emperor
down to the lowliest coolie.   Dr. Harada esti-
mates the influence of Confucianism in the following terms: "There is no doubt that Confucianism as a whole furnished flesh and blood to
the ethical life of the nation, thus playing not a
small part in the making of the faith of
Japan."[13]

C. THE FIVE VIRTUES—BENEVOLENCE, RIGHTEOUSNESS, PROPRIETY, WISDOM AND SINCERITY— JAPANESE "LOYALTY"

In addition to the formal proprieties enjoined
upon all as the foundation of orderly society,
Confucianism emphasizes certain cardinal virtues, five of which in particular Japan has
taken to herself: benevolence, righteousness,
propriety, wisdom, sincerity. The Doctrine of
the Mean mentions three "universal virtues. . .
wisdom, benevolence and fortitude.[14] To the
Chinese the one virtue which characterizes the
superior man is benevolence. In Japan one hears
the word "Loyalty" used predominantly and
embracing all these other values. As to its exact
connotation it may help the reader to know that
there is one quotation from Shakespeare which
above all others the Japanese treasure:

"To thine own self be true,
And it must follow as the night the day,
Thou canst not then be false to any man."[15]

And this is that Loyalty which the Japanese like to think constitutes the true genius of Japanese character.

That the source of such virtues was undoubtedly Confucianism few can doubt. The noble characters of such men as the Emperors Nintoku, Kenso and Ninken[16] who extolled and exemplified these virtues even before the widespread adoption of Buddhism in the land points to contacts with China earlier than any document or other historical evidence we now possess, but the similarity to the Confucian code cannot be ignored.

As for the more recent influence of these cardinal virtues, one has but to look at the wording of the Imperial Rescript on Education,[17] issued by the Emperor Meiji in 1890, to find these identical qualities extolled and taught throughout the entire educational system of the empire as the necessary foundation of modern Japanese integrity. Some of the noblest leaders in the various interests of the nation recognize these virtues as the secret of their success, and enjoin upon the youth of today a close pursuit of the same ideals. They are, indeed, beautiful and exalted principles, perhaps too lofty for men to realize in their own strength alone. At any rate, they constitute a part of the permanent spiritual heritage of the Japanese people.

D. SELF-MASTERY — THROUGH RECIPROCITY, MODERATION AND CULTURE

Confucianism has always been decidedly humanistic in its practical aspects. The Sage's own words in the Analects—"What the superior man seeks is in himself,"[18]—indicates his own assurance of self-mastery by strictly observing one's own part in the scheme of mutual propriety. Confucius seems to have believed in some type of Supreme Entity, as did the Chinese generally prior to his time[19] but the evidence is equally clear that "his own influence was to depersonalize that faith and to secularize its ethics."[20] Certain factors in the process of which one is constantly reminded in handling Confucian materials are reciprocity or mutuality, moderation or "the Mean," and culture or learning,—all of which Confucius, though modest, well exemplified, urging their realization by all.

This gospel of self-mastery served well the purpose of Buddhist missionaries in their emphasis upon the evanescence of earthly things. These lessons were even too well inculcated, for when Buddhism later became extremely superstitious and, though this-worldly in indulgence, preached an other-worldly gospel of spirits, demons, charms and incantations, it was Confucian thought which called a halt to such hypocrisy in Japan.

Self-mastery has been a doctrine with peculiar appeal to the Japanese temperament, and in no other land in the world will there be found finer personifications of this ideal. It may indeed be set forth as one of the noblest qualities in the character of the people, first because self-mastery as practiced by the Japanese has both a religious and an ethical aspect, being historically linked with both Buddhism and Confucianism; and secondly because, interpreted as triumph over selfish egoism and the unsocial spirit through the cultivation of reciprocity, moderation and culture, there is in the Confucian ideal a kinship with the Christian principle of altruism and social-mindedness as the secret of noblest self-hood.

E. "BUSHIDO", THE WAY OF THE KNIGHT

By the time Ryobu-Shinto had become well-established as the official religion in Japan, and Confucianism had imposed these aforementioned ethical obligations upon Japanese society, there was also in the process of evolution that extraordinary system of Spartan-like virtues and loyalties known as *Bushido,* or The Way of the Knight. Bushido was the outcome in a feudal era of the fused ethical principles of early Shinto, Buddhism and Confucianism.[21] Bushido held Japan to a code of high honor in an age when traditional religious convictions, and in particular the moral authority of Buddhism, were at low ebb. Bushido was the expression of as lofty an ethical consciousness as any feudal or militaristic society could evolve. Its virtues, even though never sufficiently articulate for complete classification, constituted in the heyday of feudal power, and comprise just as certainly today, "the animating spirit, the motor force, of our country."[22]

It was Dr. Nitobe who first ventured to enunciate these virtues for the Western world: rectitude or justice, courage or the spirit of daring and bearing, benevolence or the feeling of distress, politeness, veracity or truthfulness, honor, loyalty, self-control, self-sacrifice, and finally the use of the sword in defense of right.[23] Except for the last named, from the fascination of which the Japanese and many other peoples have not yet been emancipated, these are principles of which we may well say, as did Paul of the fruits of the spirit he was extolling, "If there be any virtue or if there be any praise, think on these things."[24] There are certain aspects of Bushido which should be relegated to the oblivion of outmoded ideas—and especially we recommend for this fate that pugnaciously militant spirit which in the minds of some military men seeks to find its justification in old Bushido, but which saner Japanese insist has nothing in common with the true code of the

samurai.   Nevertheless there is much in Bushido which deserves to be forever recapitulated in
the hearts and lives of her youth if Japan is to
merit and to maintain her place in "the Rising
Sun" of the world's advancement.

F. ETIQUETTE—"BETWEEN MORALS AND ART"— ALMOST RELIGION

No treatment of Confucianism's contribution
to Japanese culture can be adequate without
especial reference to Etiquette, the code of
courtesy which one breathes with the very air
in the Island Empire. Nitobe mentions politeness
as one of the virtues of a samurai.[25] Etiquette
involves more than mere manners; rather, it is
in many ways an ethic in itself. *Yamaka Soko*
who is regarded as the founder of Bushido once
wrote a treatise on practical virtue for every-
day life, and the Table of Contents discloses a
large portion of the book to be given to the consideration of "Etiquette and Dignity;" with di-
visions as follows: "Let your manners be always
quiet and courteous . . . . Be respectful at all
times . . . . Be careful what you see and hear,
what you say and how you act . . . . . . Hide
your feelings no matter how sad . . . . Be tem-
perate in your eating . . . . Be careful how you
dress. . . . Live in a house suited to your stand-
ing and furnish it accordingly. . . . Be polite
at all times, etc"[26]

In fact, Etiquette becomes for many Japanese something very like religion itself. Nitobe accords it a place in culture somewhere "between morals and art."[27] For some, indeed, it is a cult, and the consummation of Etiquette is found in the highly formal ritual of the Tea Ceremony which, presumably, none can perform whose heart and mind are not in perfect harmony with Reality.

It may seem incongruous to insist upon a definite place among the religious values in Japanese culture for a code of social habits such as Etiquette. It is not the formality, however, which the writer would extol, but the spirit back of it, an implied concern for the reality beyond the symbol, and a sympathetic regard for the interests of all those to whom courtesy is extended. It is evidence of a high degree of culture and social adaptation when a people considers regard for each other's feelings fully as much a moral obligation as, for instance, veracity. The longer one resides in Japan, the more convinced he becomes that the courtesy of the Japanese is not merely a superficial veneer to cover less wholesome thoughts and motives, but a sympathetic attitude of mind and spirit which deserves to be preserved both for the future of Japanese culture and for the sake of other peoples who may well emulate this quality. "We needs must love the highest when we see it."

G. SUPREMACY OF RI, OR SPIRIT — THE "HEART" — CLOSE APPROACH TO THEISM

It has been impossible to treat of etiquette
without occasional reference to the heart and
spirit of the Japanese. The reason is that we
are very close to the intuitive realm, the sphere
of the felt rather than of logical realities. Confucianism in Japan, if not as well in China, has
found its richest significance in sensing Reality
as the feeling, or the heart, of man objectified.
This is reflected in the *Shushi* school of Confucianism which sprang into prominence in Japan
during the 17th century, (Shushi being the Japanese pronunciation of the Chinese *Chu-Hi,* a
sage and reputed founder of this type of thought
in China at a much earlier date.)[28] This school
of moralists based their thought upon Shushi's
division of existence into *Ri* and *Ki,* the positive
and the negative, male and female, spiritual and
material, aspects of reality. This was not greatly different from the old Chinese *Yin* and *Yang*
and we have again that dual differentiation of
reality which perhaps in primitive days first
caused the Japanese to divorce the spirits of
their gods from the marvelous things-them-
selves previously worshipped as *Kami*. The difference between this primitive distinction and
the more refined state now under consideration

is that only at this comparatively late date did the Japanese begin to philosophize about it. Said *Amenomori Hoshu*, a harmonizer of religious beliefs (died 1708), "Heaven has no voice and no smell. If it has no voice, it has no shape. If it has no smell, it has no body. Buddhists call this emptiness. Taoists call it nature. Confucianists call it *Ri* (Reason)."[29] Most of the Shushi school identified Reality with the deepest intuitions of the heart. Thus *Muro Kyuso* (born 1658): "If our hearts are true we can feel the spirit of the universe."[30]

Another school of thought, the so-called *Oyomei* (Japanese pronunciation of *Wang Yang Ming*, another great Chinese Confucianist, 1472-1528),[31] carried this intuitive interpretation even farther, seeking to resolve into a unity the Chinese dualism of *Ri* and *Ki* and giving the whole a more pragmatic interpretation. The greatest exponent of this thought in Japan was *Nakae Tojiu*, who was born in the province of Omi in 1608 and is even to this day referred to as "The Sage of Omi." Like many others of the Oyomei philosophers, he was first a student of Shushi doctrine but found it not so practical, nor so satisfying as the new teaching then coming from China. His life was not long, but a disciple has said of him, "We knew his life differed from that of the common people. His face was always calm and commanded respect. Indeed, he was

the only saint-like man that Japan has ever
known."[32]

Nakae considered the spirit of man and of
the universe, which he thought of as identical
in essence and at the same time identical with
mind and conscience, to be the unifying principle of reality. For instance, he says, "Mind
controls *Ri* and *Ki,* and if so, then mind controls
the world; because they are the constituent elements of the world."[33] This smacks of pantheism, of course, yet Nakae was searching for
something more fundamental back of all and in
all and through all. Again he says, "The supreme ruler is the only great divine spirit, the
Lord and Father of heaven and earth and all
things in them . . . . . He created heaven and
earth. . . . He controls happiness and misery,
rewards the righteous, and punishes the wicked,
filling every particle of the universe, being himself omniscient and unchangeable."[34]

This is no genuine pantheism. Rather, making due allowance for translation into words
charged with Christian connotation, it seems in-
disputable that Nakae was, in thought at least,
"not far from the Kingdom of God." There
were others of this school also who found in the
noblest aspects and experiences of human life
a key to the character of the Supreme. The
names of *Kumazawa Bansan, Miwa Shitsuzai,*
and *Ogiu Sorai* suggest a grasp on Spiritual

Reality so close to the Christian conception that we wonder if they were not largely influenced by the spirit of Christianity which was just at this time making large appeal to the Japanese through the ministrations of the early Catholic missionaries. We must not, however, go too far in these assumptions. Further reading of the writings of these schools of Confucian thought convinces that they were but seeing through a glass darkly; and while no longer truly pantheistic, the Confucian philosophy, which in this period had so captivated the Japanese intelligentsia, was a form of idealistic positivism seeking further light in the quest of religious certainty.

In any event, there can be no quarrel over the inclusion of these noble, if imperfect, conceptions of the Divine life among the permanent values of the developing Japanese religious consciousness. For, let it be observed, although the authorities were systematically striving to exterminate organized Christianity in Japan,[35] they could not repress the enlarged and ennobled vision of the Highest which had, at least contemporaneously if not resultantly, found place in Japanese minds and hearts.

H. LOVE — SOCIALLY COMMENDABLE, BUT LACKING IN METAPHYSICAL SUPPORT

However, Japanese Confucian thought had

not yet arrived at the peak of its upward struggle for satisfying truth.   It did so in the ideas
and ideals of *Ito Jinsai* (born 1627), a philoso-
pher and teacher who sought to correct both
the speculative tendencies and the uncritical
sentiments of the Shushi and Oyomei schools. In
this effort Ito exhorted to a type of morality
which, with the exception of the teaching of the
early Catholic missionaries by whom directly or
indirectly he may have been influenced, excels
anything yet known in Japan. "There is no
greater virtue than to love one another, and no
worse thing than to do harm to others. This is
why Confucian teaching makes benevolence
the root of all teachings.   Benevolence is fulfilled by love only."[36] It were almost as though
Ito had said, "Greater love hath no man than
this, that a man lay down his life for his
friends."[37]   Love, self-sacrifice and service, accompanied by a vague belief in a "universal
dynamic" of benevolent mien, were finding
place in the moral consciousness of Japan. More
noble spiritual values were constantly being
added to the religious culture of these island
peoples.   An infiltration process was going on
which was to make the soil more receptive to
the seeds of Christianity, soon thereafter to be
sown again throughout Japan.

   Confucian philosophy had a magnificent opportunity to win the hearts of the Japanese

masses, had it been able. It failed. These altruistic and almost theistic interpretations of life were beautiful but they were highly speculative and unreal. Again, they did not express the true character of Confucianism which feels more at home in the Stoic atmosphere of Bushido than in the presence of universal ideals. We have discovered many elements of genuine value in Confucianism's approach to and appeal to the life of Japan; yet it is no secret that Confucianism failed to attract more than a small group of the sophisticated and the aristocratic. The philosophy of Confucianism might produce a magnificent warrior-knight — that was its greatest contribution, perhaps—but when Confucianists began to talk of heart-experiences, of God and of Love, they had far out-reached their metaphysical moorings. And if the average man could not discover the cause of the difficulty, he at least knew something was wrong, and chose not to entrust his soul to such agencies. The positivism of Confucianism, however idealistic, failed to grip the lives of the Japanese masses, though through the centuries its ethics greatly influenced their conduct and its ideals found considerable place in their religious culture. Positivistic speculation cannot take the place of religious certainty. We are told that before very long after the period of which we have been treating the various schools of Confucian thought in Japan became so intolerant of each other that they had to be officially suppressed, and that this gave rise to the next stage in the empire's religious history, the era of Modern Shinto.[38]

VII. MODERN SHINTO—THE STATE RELIGION, AND THE CULTS

We now find ourselves approaching the threshold of modern times, when Japan was persuaded to open her doors again to contact with the Western world and its culture. The very political and philosophical thought of the decades immediately preceding seem to us now to have been preparing the nation for this important decision. For a thousand years Shinto had seemed almost completely submerged by Buddhism's aggressive adaptations. Yet as early as the eighteenth century there had appeared certain thinkers and writers contending that in submitting to Buddhism's identification with and absorption of Shinto, Japan had lost much of her distinctive and vital character. Chief among these were *Kamo no Mabuchi* (1697 - 1769), *Motoori Norinaga* (1730 - 1801) and *Hirata Atsutane* (1776-1843).[1] These all advocated purging the native Japanese faith of both Confucian and Buddhist accretions, and returning to the original religious culture of the land. Like all enthusiastic lovers of "the good old days," none of these agitators realized how impossible it is to turn backward the hands of culture's timepiece. Nevertheless their propaganda had the effect of arousing popular sentiment in favor of a disestablishment of Confucianized and Shintoized Buddhism as the official religion, and the restoration of the theocracy which it was presumed had been committed to the Japanese by their own patron deities in the dim distant past.

This desire quickly became a popular passion, with the results now known in history as the Restoration of 1868. The emperor was recalled from political oblivion to be the actual, divinely-endowed and ordained head of the Japanese state, that state being thoroughly revamped into a recognized constitutional monarchy. The state religion was declared to be the ancient Shinto, the Sun Goddess being the divine ancestress of the imperial family and hence of the entire Japanese race. All the old mythology and miracle story of forgotten ages was revived and refurbished to constitute the accepted religious and political history of the empire, to which it is presumed every loyal Japanese subscribes.

A. CONSCIOUSNESS OF DIVINE DESTINY AS A NATION

Thus did Japan become a modern nation with an antiquated state religion. Here again it might seem difficult to search out and discover genuine religious values in such arbitrarily regenerated antiquarianism. Yet certain very real elements of worth have been reflected in this politico-religious transformation. In the first place, we cannot ignore the consciousness of some divinely ordained national destiny in the hearts of present day Japanese, a direct result of this restoration. The Japanese are as certain that they are a "chosen people" as were ever the Hebrews, and the implications of this in devotion to national ideas and hopes have been far-reaching and profound. There are limits beyond which such nationalism cannot avoid interference with the legitimate rights and destinies of other nations and peoples, and many of Japan's best friends feel that her statemen ofttimes hew too close to this line, if not indeed overstepping it. But it may be generally stated that insofar as patriotism serves not to limit a man's loyalty to higher goods, it is not ignoble; rather does it help to make the teaching of international cooperation and brotherhood in the interests of each and every nation the more easy of inculcation.

This consciousness of high destiny has fulfilled some such function in Japan. It has made for a remarkable degree of social solidarity among Japan's millions and a consciousness of duty thereto, whether in obedience to laws or to unwritten traditions, all of which is commendable. With the afore-mentioned reservations we therefore feel justified in giving place among the values in the religious background of Japan to this peculiar attitude of her subjects toward their nation, thought of as divinely ordained and destined for some great part in world history.[2]

B. ENLIGHTENED EMPEROR-WORSHIP — HUMAN REPRESENTATIVE OF THE KAMI

Japanese patriotism centers in the person of the emperor. In early history he became the living symbol of the gods who brought Japan into being, and for millions he has been a constant reminder of social and national duty. At certain stages of history living and dead emperors have no doubt been worshipped as themselves divine. Even today there are doubtless many among the simple-minded who do not distinguish between symbol and actuality. Yet for intelligent Japanese, emperor-worship is, as it is defined by Professor Kato, "the lofty, self-denying, enthusiastic sentiment of the Japanese people toward their august Ruler, believed to be of something divine, rendering them capable of offering up anything and everything, all dearest to them, willingly, i.e. of their own free will; of sacrificing not only their wealth or property, but their own life itself, for the sake of their divinely gracious Sovereign."[3]

Here is no mere anthropolotry; instead, we

see in it the acceptance of a personalized ideal, for as Holtom quotes from an outstanding Shinto scholar, "His person constitutes the central point at which these things (ideals) are realized here below. Therefore the Emperor is God revealed in man."[4] A royal Messiah, as it were, personifying virtue of as noble an order as has been revealed in the history of the Japanese nation. And if the future promises any loftier revelation, let it be borne in mind that each new oracle nobler than the last tends rather to fulfill than to destroy that which has served to turn men's vision heavenward. We can appreciate how much easier it is to step from one conception of incarnation to another than to be obliged to grasp the spiritual and moral interpretation of revelation with no comprehension whatever of the divine order as revealed among men.

C. TRUE PIETY — SINCERITY, "A CONDITION FOR WORSHIP"

It will be seen that such an attitude toward deity, toward the empire as a providentially conditioned order, and toward the emperor as the earthly representative of that Providence, implies a very close relationship between the gods and their Japanese children. Shinto has to this day preserved all those traditions of reverence for and familiarity with the deities which we observed to be such a marked char-

acteristic of early animistic and polytheistic
stages in its development. The effect of time
and of rubbing shoulders with Buddhism and
Confucianism seems indeed to have been a
deepening of reverence for the supernatural,
and the creation of a more genuine piety. Shinto never was and never can become a truly
ethical religion; its genius is rather, as Dr. Nitobe remarks, "a condition for worship"[5] than
a moral dynamic.

Nevertheless, there must be some preparation
of the heart which is not mere symbolic ablution before true worship and communion with
the gods, together with a successful issue of
prayer, can be assured. As early as the tenth
century a reverent prince writes, "Gods or
spirits are impartial and just in mind, pleased
only with a man's religious piety. Approach
and pray to them *with a sincere heart*, and be
sure that you will thus gain their favor."[6] And
the authors of the *Shinto-Gobusho* at a later
date are convinced that "That which pleases the
deity is virtue and sincerity, and not any number of material offerings."[7] The attitude of reverence has given rise to an inner response of
sincerity, and that in turn prompts to virtue.

D. MORAL PURITY, NOT MORE FORMAL ABLUTION, REQUIRED

Pursuing a little further the response of the

true Shintoist's heart to the gentle and decorous advances of the gods, we find a corresponding moralization of the responsibility of Purity. As early as the fifteenth century we hear *Kane-yoshi Ichijo* emphasizing that "there are two significations of purity in Shinto, one is outer purity (bodily), and the other inner purity (uprightness of heart)."[8] *Tomobe no Yasutaka* in the Tokugawa era defines ablution in no uncertain terms: "What is ablution? It is not merely the cleansing of one's body solely with lustral water; it means one's following the Right and Moral Way. Pollution means moral evil or vice. Though a man wash off his bodily filth, he will yet fail to please the deity if he restrain not his evil desires."[9]

Thus has the obligation of moral purity to some extent supplanted that of formal purity in Modern Shinto as a condition for communion with the Divine. Regardless of the conviction of many that this came about only through contact with other faiths, there can be no question that, insofar as it has penetrated the minds and hearts of the nation which worship at Shinto shrines, it is a real and abiding religious value.

E. OPTIMISM — LOVE OF NATURE — TRUST IN PROVIDENCE

Students of Japanese history and culture rejoice that with all its pessimistic restraint Bud-

dhism has not succeeded in completely repress-
ing the naturally optimistic and buoyant natures of the Japanese people. Doubtless they
needed a corrective to "sober the light-hearted
nature worshippers,"[10] and to broaden their
horizons. But the genius of the Japanese is in
their deep love of nature, their trust in the providence of natural forces, and their desire to be
beautifully natural and naturally beautiful.
This spirit is most noticeable in the joyous aban-
don of the Nipponese at cherry-blossom time, or
in the happy freedom of a shrine festival. *Kurozumi Munetada* has immortalized this spirit in
a lovely gem of literature, unfortunately impossible of English rendition as to beauty of form
and cryptic style:—

> Never lack sincerity,
> Keep in touch with life;
> Be cheerful;
> Come out from self;
> Trust in Heaven;
> Be calm of mind like a great rock
>   unmoved;
> Make your spirit courageous like
>   the morning sun."[11]

Here, in part at least, is the secret of the Japanese spirit which sees good even in disaster,
and finds occasion for trust though the earth
quake and the rocks be rent. In joy quaffing
deep of nature's bounties; in sorrow full of
hope and faith where dismay would be fatal—

here are national characteristics which one foreign religion could not stifle, nor must another
try.   They are of the essence of life abundant
through trust in a friendly universe and in cooperation with its Source and Purpose.

F. GOD-POSSESSION — THE KAMI ARE STILL VERY REAL AND INDWELLING

One of the peculiar phenomena of this familiarity with the gods in Japan is the more or less
prevalent god-possession which one encounters
occasionally, more particularly in the rural,
mountainous and unsophistocated regions. Per-
cival Lowell has given the world its best picture
of this wierd practice, together with its relationship to primitive Shinto, in the book "Occult
Japan," and Professor Anesaki supplies the
Buddhist background of the cult in his "History
of Japanese Religion."[12]   Possession by the
Kami is apparently as old as the race and as
persistent. It is, it seems, part and parcel of the
primitive conception of the gods as being capable of establishing their abode for a period of
time in the heart of man.   Even today one is
sometimes told in Japan that some eccentric
character "has a fox," the fox being identified
with the servant-deity which accompanies and
is often confused with *Inari*, the rice goodess.

At present god-possession is largely confined
to that self-identification of the worshipper with

his deities on mountain pilgrimages, at shrine festivals, and in other Shinto observances. The universality of this experience helps to explain the remarkable solidarity and cohesiveness of the Japanese; they unite as a man in such worship. Its vitality is attested to and accounted for by Lowell in concluding that "in Shinto god-possession, we are viewing the actual incarnation of the ancestral spirit of the race. The man (thus possessed) has once more temporarily become his own indefinitely great-great-grandfather. . . . If these his ancestors were gods in the past, gods they are that descend to embodiment today."[13]

It is the writer's conviction that here too is a religious value worthy of preservation. Although, as reference to the Old Testament substantiates, such phenomena are frequently accompanied by the unmoral, and even immoral, excesses of fanaticism, nevertheless the point for our observation here is that every religion of the spirit seeks to incarnate its genius in the life of man, to make that spirit personal and real, and to secure its abode in the hearts of its devotees. Shinto has succeeded in producing such a conviction of the reality of the gods, tested by their felt presence in man's inner experience.

G. THEISM — CERTAIN CULTS EVEN WORSHIP "SUPREME DEITY"

This felt presence of the gods in human hearts has lent itself throughout Japanese history to rationalizations congenial to various religious viewpoints.   Buddhism and Confucianism have both had a moulding effect upon the popular concepts of deity.   There is also reason to believe that Christian influence is not entirely lacking.   Evidence of such infiltration will be considered under a later topic, but we merely point out here that in the past few centuries, and in particular in recent years, Shinto thought has brought its adherents almost if not completely to a monotheistic conception of the Source of Purity and Life.[14] As early as the seventeenth century a Shinto scholar asks, "What is Deity?" and replies in transcendent terms: "The Deity is the Absolute. It transcends human words, which are of a relative nature. It is incomprehensible, and yet it permeates all things. It is everywhere."[15] Again, in the nineteenth century a Shinto high priest sings in terms half-pantheistic and yet more ultimate:

There is no place on this wide earth,—
Be it the vast expanse of Ocean's waste,
Or peak of wildest mountain, sky-caressed—
In which the ever-present power divine
In every force of nature's not a shrine.[16]

And early in the present century the great Emperor Meiji voiced in a poem a genuinely theistic sentiment:

> With the unseen God
> Who seeth all secret things
> In the silence,
> Communes from the earth below
> The heart of man sincere.[17]

Today the thirteen religious (i.e. non-political) sects of Shinto are all more or less theistic, and some of them beyond question monotheistic and personalistic.   The founder of one of the oldest of these sects, *Kurozumi Munetada* (1779-1849) says, "The origin of all lives of the universe is *Amaterasu-Omikami*, the mother-god, whose sunny spirit pervades the universe, giving birth to all things by her light and heat, and ceases not to nurture them all."[18] In the English reference book published for propaganda purposes by the officials of the popular *Tenrikyo* sect we read, "These ten gods (of creation and sustenance), all working in harmonious operation forever in a body for the creation and protection of men and the world, are considered and worshipped as one, and are most reverently called 'Tenri no Mikoto' (The Heavenly Reason-Deity)."[19]

This certainly is a far cry from the primitive polytheism of early Shinto.   Here is simply another highly evolved religious value which

holds place in the lives of a large proportion of
the Japanese people, and is worthy of perpetuation in whatever transition Japan is asked to
make to a more advanced level of religious and
social thinking. The monotheistic conception is
not easily created where there is no tendency to
such thought; where such an inclination exists
it should be treasured, nurtured, and made the
foundation of a nobler religious and ethical
order.

H. UNIVERSAL PURPOSE — JAPAN'S MISSION TO THE WORLD

Finally, Shinto has within it the vision of a
universal order. That this in its more prevalent
aspects is not always a worthily conceived ideal
cannot be denied. Shinto as the "duty of the
Japanese people . . . . to spread that religion
and culture until the Emperor of Japan shall
become the supreme emperor and spiritual
ruler of the world,"[20] is the dream of pure jin-
goism, concurred in by only the most fanatical
patriots and Shintoists, and not even to be considered seriously. But in Kurozumi's moralized
universalism there is larger worth:

> The noblest attribute of life,
> Most surely is Sincerity of mind,
> That shines serenely through the whole
>   world's strife,
> And man to man in brotherhood doth bind.[21]

It would seem that true Shinto has been
handicapped and fettered by its modern identification with a political order which seeks its
own perpetuation through religious sanctions.
As a religion, Shinto has spiritual values which
outweigh its faults; as the backbone of Japanese imperialism Shinto is no better—or worse—
than any other state cult used for political ends.
K. Kanokogi puts this paradox in precise form:
"Diffused, Shinto is an active force impelling
the nation forward, as an ardent love of the fa-
therland and of the whole. From this flow all
virtues: altruism, sacrifice, loyalty, etc. But
concentrated, it would become a contemptible
chauvinism, and turning its back on the whole
world, would sink to a narrow provincialism,
fettering the nation in its cultural endeavors
and obstructing its onward and forward march.
For its lift, its longing for more, would be
lost."[22]

VIII. MODERN BUDDHISM—A
RENAISSANCE

With the revival of Shinto and the restoration
of the emperor, Buddhism was forcibly dis-
established as the favored religion in Japan,
and every effort was made to purge the old
Shinto faith and its shrines of one thousand
years' accumulation of Buddhist influence.[1]
Buddhism, thus thrown upon its own resources,
began to decline, and for a time seemed destined to pass away even as it had done in India and
to an extent in China and Korea. But Japanese
Buddhism possesses a certain power of persistence and continual rejuvenation not known in
other Asiatic lands. With the coming of contact with the outside world it became apparent
that Buddhism was not expiring but, speaking
more particularly of certain aggressive sects,
was preparing for a renaissance which would
put Buddhism again very much to the fore
among the religions of Japan. That alertness
has continued to this day, and certain features
stressed therein must be taken into account if
we wish an adequate picture of the values in the
religious outlook of modern Japan.

A. THE MYSTIC, ESOTERIC ELEMENT IN LIFE

First, we must note that peculiar mystic esoterism which resides in Buddhism in all its
forms. For the Buddhist there is a state of
"spiritual peace which comes of perfected
knowledge and the subjugation of all passions."[2] This is not only true in the realm of religious phenomena; one well versed in the art of
fencing and archery points out that such a sense
of at-one-ness with the underlying principles of
the physical universe, for instance, puts one in
command of new resources even in the exact co-
ordination of mind, eye and arm required for
skill with the Japanese sword or the bow.[3]
Buddhism has succeeded in indoctrinating its
devotees with the importance of that mystic adjustment to life without which fullest self-realization is not possible. Philosophical Buddhism's
means of accomplishing this has been by
resort to silence and meditation. Even the most
popular sects, the "Pure Land" group, i.e. those
assuring salvation through mere faith, have
nevertheless large place reserved for silence
and systematized meditation upon the deeper
aspects of existence. One school of Buddhist
thought, the *Zen-shu*, places its major emphasis
upon meditative esoterism. Even as it gave rise
to that revival of Confucianism which contributed to the overthrow of corrupt and superstitious Buddhism from its seat of might and pride,

so is Zen yet today stressing this element of silence and meditation as the chief requisite to Enlightenment.[4]

Is there an esoteric element in life, and is meditative silence one means of attaining at-one-ness with the universe? A recent biographer of Napoleon contends that only by reference to that Oriental idea of the spiritual continuity of life into which Napoleon entered by intuitive memory, or as Plato calls it "ana-mnesis" (mystical remembrance), can one explain Napoleon's uncanny insight into the underlying circumstances and issues of a given problem.[5] Regardless of the aptness of the observation concerning Napoleon, this author seems to have properly appraised the Oriental mind. It does assume the mystic unity and continuity of life, and Buddhism does assert that by conditioning the self of senses and passions, through communication with inner sources of power, the faithful may enter into the secret of that unity and continuity.

Buddhism has gone farther than any other religion in exploring this apprehension of the mystic and eternal through meditation. Henri Bergson, another French genius, has called the attention of the West to the realm of intuition and "sympathetic integration" with reality. His discoveries in the psychical sphere convince us that many of the mystic values of Buddhism, now so much a part of the Japanese nature, should be preserved in anticipation of greater future conquest of these realms of inner consciousness.

B. AGGRESSIVE PIETY AND DEVOTION TO "THE FAITH"

When these realms of the inner life shall have been explored and charted we shall better understand that peculiar blend of piety and aggressive devotion to Buddhism so characteristic of those sects which evolved in the latter days of the so-called Buddhist era, and have taken on added vigor during the Renaissance of which we are now treating. Undoubtedly the prototype and hero of this devotion to and zeal for Buddhist principles in preference to the many "foreign" ideas which have been pouring into Japan in recent centuries is the fiery-hearted prophet of the thirteenth century, *Nichiren* (Sun-Lotus, 1222-1282).[6] So much related in spirit to the Old Testament, Nichiren is yet strangely modern. His zeal and vigor in defense of the *Saddharma Pundarika* sutra (Lotus Gospel[7]) have communicated themselves not only to his immediate followers but even to those of other sects which, while Nichiren lived, were his opponents.

Nichiren may properly be called the Father of the Buddhist "Church." Concerning the prophet's vision of a world-wide Catholic Buddhism, Dr. Anesaki says, "Japan, for Nichiren, was the country where the Universal Buddhist Church was to have its central seat; but Japan in an ideal sense meant the whole world—transformed in the light of the Scripture. Nichiren deemed himself to be the man sent by Buddha to open the way for the transformed world, the messenger of Buddha, an incarnation of the Truth."[8]

The spirit of the present-day renaissance of Buddhism, it may be said, is a revival of the ardour of Nichiren. The Nichirenites are the most militant sect in Japan today. Their traditional rivals, the Amida Buddhists, have likewise imbibed deeply of Nichiren's qualities, and even for that group of young zealots who maintain a Young Men's Buddhist Association in most cities, high schools and colleges in the empire, Nichiren is the symbol of aggressive defense of Buddhist traditions against the onslaughts of other religious and anti-religious propaganda.

Some may question the propriety of Christian praise of Buddhist piety and devotion. Yet from the standpoint of pure sportsmanship one rejoices to see loyalty and courage even among one's rivals. For, even where evangelists seek to win converts from Buddhism to the Christian cause it is discovered that those who are most easily convinced of Christianity's superiority are often the most readily tossed about by other doctrinal winds as well. Again, with the spread of materialism and secularism in the modern world the conviction has come to many that advocates of an idealistic interpretation of life, and embracing somewhat similar ethical standards, have more in common against a mutual foe than the importance of any differences of interpretation among themselves. It is for these reasons that the writer is assured that the spirit of aggressive piety which to a large extent characterizes the modern revival of Buddhism in Japan constitutes a bulwark of idealism in an uncertain age, and is therefore to be highly evaluated in any survey of the religious culture of the Japanese.

C. EMPHASIS UPON CITIZENSHIP AND SOCIAL RESPONSIBILITY — PRACTICAL ETHICS

Pursuing just a little farther this point of mutual values in Japanese Buddhism and Christianity, we discover much in the ethical realm which may be said to be common ground. Paradoxical though it may seem, modern Buddhism while seeking to retain the sense of the mystical which has characterized it in the past strives also today to prepare its devotees for the fullest possible adaptation to and citizenship in modern life. In this, all sects have been greatly influenced by *Shinran Shonin* (1174-1268)[9] and

his followers of the so-called *Shin-shu* (Shin or
True-sect) of the Pure Land School of Mahayana Buddhism. The great teacher of Shinran,
Honen Shonin (born 1130)[9] had taught the
availability of salvation to all who took the
"Nembutsu" (Namu-Amida-Butsu) in faith upon their lips. Shinran went a logical step beyond
his master's position; he was prepared to re-
nounce not only the essentially pessimistic and
unsocial doctrines of old-order Buddhism, but
their practical implications as well. If the act
of faith alone saves a man, why then worry
about the renunciation of the things of this life?
Better for even the priest to take a positive attitude toward life, marry, raise a family, eat
meat, and live a normal life in the community,
trusting in Amida to ultimately save, and looking upon good works as having no saving merit
but as the expected fruits of faith.[10]

The Buddhism which has revived to boldly
face a new and modern day is, for the most part,
of this general character. Prof. J. Takakusu is
convinced that "if there is a Buddhism most
suitable for Japan it is this True-sect."[11] It is
this sect whose priests are most alert to help
solve the great social problems of Japan today.
It is *Shinshu* which sends its priests abroad for
study and observation. It is this True-sect which
has such a strong following in Hawaii and also
has temples and congregations on the American

Pacific coast. It is Shinshu which adopts from
Christianity, or from any other source, methods
and ideas which may be employed to advantage
to inculcate Buddhist doctrines. The Shin sect
is, again, Christianity's greatest competitor today, for it meets Christianity on somewhat its
own ground as a social and moral force for
human uplift and personal salvation.[12]

The modern Buddhist moral ideal then, consists, according to Dr. Anesaki, "in practicing
all the precepts of morality in their essence and
spirit, regardless of circumstances and conditions."[13] The immense value of such a moral
sense and of even an approximate realization of
such an ideal, all must see. If, however, considered historically and confirmed by present-
day observation, the power to realize the ideal
seems less than sufficient, we have but once
more in our search for values happened upon
the hiatus so common between ideals and prac-
tices in the history of religions. Yet, if the dis-
crepancy between Buddhist ideals and the
moral level at which Buddhists traditionally live
seems even greater today than in the earlier
days of Buddhism's influence in Japan, and
more discouraging,[14] it will be with the greater
hope and expectancy that we turn now to the
evidence of the infusion of Japanese culture
with Christian ideals and with power for their
realization.

IX. CHRISTIANITY

No adequate picture of the religious outlook
of the Japanese people today could fail to give
attention to the influence and contribution of
Christianity. The known history of this relationship begins with the coming of Francis Xavier
and his fellow missionaries to Japanese shores
a little before the middle of the sixteenth century. But Christian influence upon Japanese
thought may have antedated this contact by almost a thousand years. Dr. Armstrong has held
that Nestorian Christianity may have had a definite share in *The awakening of faith in Mahayana* in China shortly after 635 A.D. when
Christians from Persia were known to have been
working there. The book by the above title has
generally been ascribed to Ashvagosha in an
earlier age, but there is a strong inclination
among certain scholars now to attribute it to a
much later period and to another author, probably a Chinese "directly or indirectly influenced by the growing Christian movement.[1]" Again,
Armstrong produces evidence of the presence
of Persian Christians in Japan during the Nara

era (621 - 782 A.D.). He quotes Professor
Yamamoto's first volume on "The History of
Christianity in Japan":—"We read in the chronicles of the Emperor *Shomu* in the *Shoku-Ni-
hongi* that on a certain day of July in the eighth
year of Tempyo three Chinese and one Persian
came to Japan with *Ason Nakatomi* who had
been to China as a vice-envoy, and also that in
November the emperor conferred rank on *Kobo
Tochyo* a Chinese and *Limitsu* a Persian."[1] These,
Professor Yamamoto is convinced, were Nestorian missionaries in Japan, and he further feels
assured that this early Christian influence was
responsible for the establishment of many hu-
mane and charitable institutions in Japan heretofore thought to have been founded under the
aegis of Buddhism. Yamamoto even suggests
that an empress's name in this period was *Komyo*
(Great Light), the identical phrase used by the
Chinese for Nestorianism.

Be that as it may—and scholarship must discover much more evidence before any such hy-
pothesis can be accepted as established—we
may nevertheless assume on the basis of many
recent discoveries in Persia, Syria, India, Tibet,
China, Korea, and Japan, that the East and the
West, so long thought of as utterly divorced in
life and thought since the beginning of time,
have in reality throughout history and particularly since the opening of the Christian era,

experienced constant interchange of ideas and customs. Nestorian Christianity may very probably have had a not insignificant share in that process, and we may discover that much which has made the Mahayanist so different from Hinayanist Buddhism and more like Christianity—e.g in the universalization of the ideal of Justice and Mercy, the conception of the Eternal Buddha, a doctrine of Salvation by faith, belief in heaven and hell, etc.—is, indeed, due to penetrations of Buddhist thought by Christian ideas, as many scholars have suggested. Again, it may all be a figment of the imagination, stimulated by the desire that it might be so. Hence we must not put too much weight on such as yet not thoroughly established theories.[2]

When we turn to the influence of the early European missionaries and their converts, however, we are nearer our own time and the data are more reliable. Many of the theistic, even monotheistic ideas which we have noted as expressed by later Shinto, Buddhist and Confucian thinkers, have undoubtedly been colored to some extent by direct or indirect contact with Christian beliefs. We have, for example, the the words of *Kumazawa Bansan* (born 1619), disciple of *Nakae Tojiu*, in which he at first regarded Christianity "as a disease that takes hold of the body itself; the roots of this disease lie in the superstition and poverty of the peo-

ple," but later says he regards it as "superior to
Buddhism, being more reasonable, and having
a more clever method of propaganda." He even
thinks Confucianism will "be vanquished by
Christianity."[3]   Yet, even though Kumazawa
went this far in recognizing Christianity's superiority to other religions, and moreover accepted
in large part as his own Nakae Tojiu's religious
and ethical principles, he preferred to abide by
the faith of his fathers, perhaps a very politic
thing to do in those days when Christianity was
being suspected and suppressed.

We are not so much concerned, however,
with evidence of either plagiarism or acknowl-
edged acceptance of Christian principles by
non-Christian faiths, as with the actual existence of valuable elements drawn from different sources to the religious culture. It was for
convenience and with regard for chronological
development that we have proposed to consider
these values under the heads of the faiths, or
philosophies from which they have emerged
and appeared among the Japanese. It is therefore fitting and proper that we should now designate such of the Christian values as have impressed themselves upon Japanese character
and consciousness to date.

A. THE FATHERHOOD OF GOD — A THEISTIC ABSOLUTE

We have seen emerging in the Japanese mind

a conception of God very close to the theistic idea held by the Christians. We need not hold that it is a thoroughly monotheistic conception. Yet today a recognized term for "God" will be found in common use among all classes and types of Japanese people; and though worship and sacrifice may be offered before many deities, these various gods are, in the phraseology of the popular Tenrikyo sect of Shinto, "considered and worshipped as one."[4] It is highly significant that one of the widely known dictionaries of the Japanese language[5] defines the word *Kami* as: "(1) a spirit which is thought to exist invisibly, with unlimited supernatural power of good or ill to punish crime and reward virtue in human beings; an object of religious trust or fear; (2) the honorific name given to rulers previous to the reign of Jimmu; (3) the name applied to spirits enshrined in Shinto shrines; (4) the Christian God, the almighty and omnipresent creator and ruler; the Heavenly Ruler; (5) the spirits of the dead in Shinto funeral ceremonies; (6) that which transcends human understanding." Professor Anesaki refers to the Western and Christian influence reflected in the writings of Hirata Atsutane (1776-1843) who introduced a decidedly monotheistic conception of the divine into the Shinto beliefs. He also speaks of the founders of the *Kurozumi* and *Tenri* sects as defenders of "almost pure monotheism in a very simple and devout form."[6]

In thinking in terms of divine fatherhood there has also been a further marked acceptance of the Christian viewpoint by the Japanese in recent years. The Emperor Meiji (died 1912) gave utterance to certain sentiments in poetry, as we have seen,[7] and also in prose which reveal a profound faith in the paternal providence of the Supreme. "Because of the existence of God who guides all men, the world is being civilized in an unprecedented way. God's authority is seen protecting the world in time of need."[8] In commenting on the emperor's ideas, Dr. Genchi Kato says, "Coming to know God to be like this, one experiences for the first time the exquisite part of religion. It is due to this form of theism that Christ could see the glory of God revealed even in a lily and in a falling sparrow."[8]

Perhaps it is too much to expect our Buddhist friends to completely discard their rich symbolism of over two milliennia of development. But what we may expect more and more of in the future is the identification of the Fatherhood of God with something most akin to it in their own thought, and a moralization and spiritualization of that Buddhist concept in keeping therewith. Thus we find an earnest and devout Buddhist priest rationalizing as follows: "The absolute Buddha, omnipresent in all things, or Truth, corresponds to God, Father, Creator of all things, or primary Truth. This Father corresponds to the Law-body of Buddha and I believe these two are different in name but the same in reality."[9] For our purpose, regardless of the truth or falsity of this assumption, what we see here is an accomplished penetration of Buddhist doctrine with Christian meaning, a phenomenon of which every student in comparing earlier with present-day Buddhism becomes aware. The Christian idea of God as Father and as One Lord over heaven and earth has captured the Japanese imagination, and the native faiths have, for the most part, determined to trim their sails accordingly.

B. THE WORTH OF PERSONALITY — FREEDOM AND BROTHERHOOD

Buddha's conviction that what we today regard as the soul, the self, the personality, was the fundamental source of the great evils of existence,[10] led him to repudiate the self and to urge its complete abnegation—instincts, passions, desires, hopes, and everything that smacked of cravings unsatisfied. The Mahayana doctrine, however, placed larger value on the individual, and Buddhism in Japan concerned itself through the centuries with as positive an interpretation of life as could possibly be superimposed upon an essentially negative philosophy.

We have seen what *Dengyo Daishi* and *Kobo Daishi* in the Heian era (794 A.D. fol.) promulgated in the direction of a fuller, more abundant life of identification with the Eternal.[11] In the latter stages of this era and early in the Kamakura age, we find *Honen* and *Shinran*, founders of the Jodo (Pure Land) doctrines, advocating an even more positive view of this life and definite hope for the future.[12] Though mixed with metaphysical notions quite inadmissible today, these were all gestures in the direction of a higher evaluation of human personality. So forward looking were these leaders of thought in fact that their successors failed to comprehend their idealism, and Buddhism as a moral force shortly fell into moral decay, finally being ejected as the efficial religion of the land.

Meanwhile Confucianism had been seeking to meet the personal and social needs of the nation with an intuitive philosophy to support the great ethical principles which Japan had long since adopted from China. Although primarily humanitarian in emphasis, this philosophy also failed to affect any appreciable enhancement in consciousness of personal human values.[13]

Passing for the moment the influence of the early Christian movement we next see a revival of Shinto with its reappraisal of emperor worship, a doctrine calculated to submerge all personal interests in promotion of the national good,[14] and hence incapable of enhancing the value of individual personality in the religious consciousness of Japan.

Thus, wherever we search in the history of Japanese religion down to the threshold of the modern age, we find little of emphasis upon the worth of the individual man or woman in society. And yet today one frequently reads words such as the following from the pen of Dr. Anesaki, a most distinguished Buddhist scholar with a Confucian ethical background and a political outlook favorable to Shinto: "The moral and intellectual perfection of a personality is, in spite of the doctrine of the non-ego, the highest aim of Buddhist morality."[15] And again, "In summarizing positively the highest aim of Buddhist morality, we might say it consists in entering into the communion of all the Buddhas and saints through realizing the one-ness of eternity in one's own personality."[16] This may be interpreted Buddhistically, doubtless, as Dr. Anesaki proceeds to do, but surely we are aware here of the use of a peculiarly Western terminology, if not actually of Western and Christian ideas. And when, in addition to this, we discover this renowned scholar advancing from this affirmation of personality to consideration of steps leading to a Buddhist program of social amelioration and world brotherhood—an aspect of Christianity which he very much admires,

we are convinced that such an assumption of
human freedom is neither an implication of the
native paternalistic polytheism, nor of Confucian
moral philosophy, nor of Shinto thought, nor
yet of Mahayana Buddhism, however divorced
the latter from its original Indian associations.
Such attitudes and hopes were either borrowed
from the Christian Gospel following its earliest
introduction to Japan four hundred years ago,
or have grown up during the more recent contacts with Christianity, or both.

In any event, the Japanese today almost uni-
versally believe in the intrinsic worth of the human spirit and this conviction has had large
part in the remoulding of Japanese society
along more wholesome social lines.   Ancestor
worship has contributed somewhat to the evaluation of selfhood, to be sure. Mahayana Buddhism has made heroic efforts to turn its un-
wieldy doctrines to the enhancement of personality. Confucianism has laid an ethical foundation for a lofty structure of personal and eternal
values. But the mind of Japan today is closer
to the Christian conception of the worth of the
human soul in the eyes of the Almighty than to
the metaphysics of any other religious faith.

C. ACTIVE LOVE — SUPPORTED BY UNIVERSAL SPIRIT

We have seen how close *Ito Jinsai* approached
to the Christian concept of Love.[17] Some have

felt that the affinity was more than a coincidence. Be that as it may, we are aware of a spirit of active love in Japan today for which Christianity may be said to be largely responsible. One of the spheres in which this new and vigorous spirit is most evident is in the attempts being made to improve the unhappy social conditions of modern Japan, a work in which Dr. Toyohiko Kagawa has rendered such distinguished service. Concerning this characteristic of the Western faith, Professor Anesaki remarks, "Christianity has always, since the beginning of the new age, been eminent in social work and its leadership still rests on that, in spite of the rather insignificant number of its converts."[18]

We shall not here attempt to show how the more aggressive sects of the other faiths have sought to imitate the active social aspects of the Christian program—hospitals, settlements, reform legislations, temperance and purity movements, etc.[19]   There is, however, great significance in the manner in which the leaders of Japan's moral life are seeking to integrate the spirit of love into the fabric of Japanese thought and custom.   A recent writer refers to the way in which this Christian idea of love has been incorporated in the educational subject-matter of the empire.[20] Text books and teachers' manuals draw heavily from Biblical and other Christian sources, and these references almost invariably extol love as the ground-work of human relationships. Excerpts from the Sermon on the Mount are frequent, and the reader becomes keenly conscious of "the difference in tone in the books from what it was . . . . . fifteen to twenty years ago, . . . much more about sacrifice for others, love of enemies, the democratic spirit."[20] What are we to presume when in a public school a play is given in which the Creator is made to say to all the animals, "I am the All-Father! God is Love."!

Apart from public school education one finds in the most popular magazines in Japan large space given to illustrated Biblical and other Christian material extolling love and human brotherhood on universal grounds, and such moving pictures as "The Sign of the Cross," "The King of Kings" and "The Ten Commandments" have never failed to draw capacity crowds. Again, one of the most widely known books in Japan is the inter-denominational hymn book; it will be found in almost every enlightened home, whether Christian or not. Doubtless the most commonly known hymn is "Kami wa Ai-nari," (God is Love), which one may hear on the lips of many who perhaps are not conscious of ascribing praise to the Christian God. We have repeatedly heard of the adoption and adaptation of Christian hymns to suit Buddhist needs, and one that is frequently taught to children in their Sunday schools is,

"Buddha loves me, this I know,
For the Lotus tells me so."

Shinto likewise seeks to appropriate this active spirit of universal love which, until comparatively recent times, was foreign to the genius of Japanese religion. Look for a moment again at Tenrikyo, which Aston said had almost a million-and-a-half adherents in 1894,[21] and today may have as many as five million. In the Tenrikyo publication previously cited we read, "Sincerity is an attitude of an awakened spirit thoroughly cleansed from dusts as well as quite free from a bad fate. Spirit is your veritable self and is sincerity itself. Sincerity, when it works naturally, is love. Love therefore is the will of your spirit. Your spirit, being a part of God's spirit, i.e. the will of your spirit, is therefore the pery will of God the Almighty."[22]

These are not isolated phenomena, for the explicit emphasis upon love noted in Japanese schools and in other educational media may be said to be the result of a purposeful policy on the part of the Imperial Department of Education which determines the character of all secular instruction and seeks publicly to promote the official religion of Shinto.[23] There is a serious effort being made to imbue the popular religions of the land with a more humanitarian out-

look.   Active, universal love, not originally a
part of the religious culture of Japan, has come
in recent decades to appeal acutely to the consciousness of her people.   It is a religious value
of highest importance, for the emergence of
which Christianity may accept a large share of
responsibility.

D. SALVATION — NOT ESCAPE FROM, BUT TRIUMPH OVER, EVIL

We have glimpsed the early Shinto view of
life as fellowship with the hallowed spirits,
little however being thought concerning moral
fitness for eternal communion therewith.   Buddhism, with the aid of Confucian ethics, brought
a new consciousness of moral responsibility, for
which the Mahayana teaching devised an elaborate system of retribution.   The gradual emergence of the assurance of a Western Paradise
for the blessed was also a part of Buddhism's
evolution in Eastern Asia, as was also the
conception of Bodhisattva-hood, which declines
or postpones the blessings of Nirvana for the
opportunity of returning to or remaining on
earth as a saviour of humanity.   The approxi-
mation here to the Christian view of salvation
has been noted, as has also the fact that Japanese Buddhism is, nevertheless, constantly embarrassed by the incompatibility of its essential
philosophy with such doctrines.   This has cast

a pessimistic shroud around Buddhism wherever it has sought to exalt life. The world is
necessarily evil, and salvation has been conceived by Buddha and by all his disciples as escape
from evil and suffering—and this is, in the last
analysis, a selfish desire. Thus has Buddhism's
charge against the fundamental selfishness of
other forms of salvation lost much of its force,
with the result that Mahayana Buddhism has
advanced as far as it can toward the positive
interpretation of life hereafter without completely repudiating its philosophical antecedents.

But forever must Buddhism, so long as it is
Buddhism, be so embarrassed. The seeker after
Enlightenment through promised blessings and
joys is inevitably confronted by an inexorably
evil world. Then, when Buddhism has been reduced to its self-consistent essentials, Salvation
consists in "a form of higher ethical life in
obedience to the commandments and maxims of
Buddhism."[24] That is all! There is in arriving
at this state, whether by self-abnegation or by
meditation or by deeds of mercy or simply by
following the moral laws, a glow of satisfaction comparable in kind perhaps, if not in degree, to the emotional consciousness of being
"saved" with which Christians are familiar. Yet
after all, one is merely saved *from* the evils of
environment and of self, and not *to* any other

positive form of existence. Only may the philosophical Buddhist say that he has been "enlightened" and is living on a higher plane of moral excellence unaffected by the miserable conditions of life about him. If he harks back to the Indian antecedents of his faith, he is saved from the cycle of rebirth in a lower form of life—as a dog or a snake—due to sin and evil. If a Mahayanist, he may be saved to save others. But to what and for what others are to be saved Buddhism cannot consistently answer more than this: themselves in turn to escape from the evil world for the sake of helping others to escape, ad infinitum.

Japanese Buddhism has, however, said more than this. Regardless of consistency, it has presumed to speak authoritatively about a state of love and assurance which redeems and ennobles life from the plane of the miserable and low to something eternally beautiful and significant. Thus a modern Buddhist teacher can assure his readers: "The worse a man is the more Buddha pities him; the more estranged a man is the more Buddha loves him: such is Buddha. . . . The meaning of life is thoroughly understood when one is led to the light of Buddha and experiences a new birth."[25] On this

Armstrong comments: *"Chikazumi Jokwan,* in his method, in the emphasis he lays upon experience, in his conception of evil and salvation from sin, seems clearly to illustrate the penetration of Buddhism by Christian thought, even though some of the historic Buddhist illustrations scarcely support his moral emphasis."[24]

E. IMMORTALITY — CONSERVATION OF THE VALUES IN PERSONALITY

Christians cannot think of salvation apart from the recognition by the Supreme One of the intrinsic worth of personality, as well as of the innate yearnings of the human spirit for a noble and eternal life. We have seen earlier that Shinto from the first assumed an assurance of fellowship after death with the gods and with departed loves ones and heroes; and that popular Buddhism was indoctrinated with this uncritical belief. Certain Buddhist leaders thereupon took over this assumption, moralized it somewhat, and developed it into a thoroughly un-Buddhistic but none-the-less substantial dogma. That development has not yet ceased, for today we find unmistakable evidence of a popular belief in a future life closely resembling, if not actually modelled after, the Christian view of immortality. Dr. Reischauer gives the testimony of an ignorant old Buddhist believer which may be said to be quite characteristic of the faith of the masses:—

"I am old and I am a woman, and it is not expected that a woman will know much of such

subjects, but I will tell you what thoughts I
have. I am weak and sinful, and have no hope
in myself; my hope is all in Amida Buddha. I
believe him to be the Supreme Being. Because
of the wickedness of man and because of human
sorrow, Amida Buddha became incarnate and
came to earth to deliver man; and my hope and
the world's hope is to be found only in his suffering love. He has entered humanity to save
it; and he alone can save. He constantly watch-
es over and helps all who trust in him. I am not
in a hurry to die, but I am ready when my time
comes; and I trust that through the gracious
love of Amida Buddha I shall then enter into
the future life which I believe to be a state of
conscious existence, and where I shall be free
from sorrow. I believe that he hears prayer,
and that he has guided me thus far; and my
hope is only in his suffering love."[26]

Making all necessary allowance for the probable receipt of this testimony by a Christian,
and for its translation into orthodox Christian
terminology, there can be little questioning this
evidence of the penetration of popular Buddhist
thought by Christian ideology. Our concern is
not so much with the medium of this infusion—
whether through priests who plagiarized or
from other contacts with Christianity. What is
most important is this: (1) in Japan today we
find strongly entrenched and highly significant
religious values having to do with belief in a
God who is Father of all men and who has given
His creatures personalities of such inherent

worth as to urge us to noble fellowship and brotherhood each with all other human beings in
that spirit of active love which is sensed to be
the highest quality in the universe; and (2) the
Japanese, for the most part, and with few exceptions as to the type of faith embraced, expect this God of Love to recognize the intrinsic
values bound up in these human personalities of
ours, and to satisfy our deepest yearnings for
which He alone is responsible, by a conservation
of our selves, our spirits, our personalities—i.e.
whatever is of indestructible value—in eternal
fellowship with Himself, and with those who
have gone before. Any less magnanimous treatment of His creatures would constitute a repu-
diation of the very qualities of Eternal Justice,
Mercy and Love which have through the centuries gradually found place even in the Buddhist conception of the Divine. Dr. Harada
speaks for all the world, but is thinking particularly of Japan, when he says, "The heart re-
vives faith in immortality faster than the intel-
lect destroys it."[27]

F. INDWELLING PRESENCE URGING TO COOPERATION
WITH THE DIVINE

It is in the doctrine of the indwelling of the
Divine spirit that Christianity may seem most at
variance with the native religious ideas of
Japan. We have seen, however, that Shinto has

not been averse to a belief in god-possession; to
this day among the ignorant, people are often
said to be "possessed" by this or that spirit.
Universal education has led away from such
superstition, to be sure, but where there is not
too much sophistication accompanying the "new
learning" there is still a wholesome regard for
the intercourse that may take place—indeed,
the possible intimacy—between the living and
the spirit of the departed and other deities: to
wit, the widespread observance of the *O-bon*
festival when Japan's ancestors, both celestial
and human, return for a few days of fellowship
in the homes and hearts of their descendents.

Buddhism's compromise with these conceptions we have also noted. Mahayana's only concern was that this "communion" be thought of
as with the Eternal Buddha, rather than with or
through Amaterasu Omikami, the native Sun-
goddess. More recently Buddhists have seen fit
to propose a similar compromise with Christianity. God may be identified with the Eternal
Buddha, the historic incarnate Christ with Gautama who also came to save men, and the indwelling Spirit with the "reward-body" of
Buddha.[28] Buddhist priests and scholars quite
commonly today make this comparison, and one
Buddhist professor comments:

"As we see in the psychology of man that in-
tellect, emotion and will are nothing but three

phases of one mind, so here it is evident that the three bodies of Buddha and the three persons of God are respectively three phases of one Buddha and of one God. . . . . I, as one of the Buddhists, hope that these two great religions may be unified into a still greater and more ideal one."[29]

Yet if, as we have seen, the underlying Buddhist concept of Reality differs so widely from that of Christianity, it follows that Christ and Buddha cannot be identified in character and significance without violence to the historic nature of both. Even granting that the Buddhist idea of God has greatly altered into something akin to the Christian conception, it cannot follow that Gautama Buddha, the agnostic Stoic of the East, can be metamorphosed into the Christ, thought of either as the Revealer of the Father-God to man, or as the Indwelling Presence which Christians refer to as the Holy Spirit.

While theologies influence society and mould character, it is equally true that the mores of a people and their social institutions help to determine theologies and religious convictions. Changes in Buddhist ideas in Japan have been, at least in part, adaptations to existing religious conditions. The more progressive sects of Buddhism are even today, as we have seen, making adjustments so as to be better able to help create a consciousness of the abiding presence of the Eternal Buddha in the hearts of all men.

All this may be to the good; so much gain for a spiritual interpretation of the universe. Its beneficial results are most apparent, however, when there is no disposition to investigate or be critical of the antecedents of this faith. When such searching for origins and for reasons does occur—as when, for instance, a Japanese student's mind is aroused by higher education— the result, upon discovering that an attempt has been made deliberately to build the structure of a positive religious faith upon the foundation of a negative philosophy, is inevitably disillusionment, and sometimes despair.

Full of truth and light though the Lotus Gospel, *Saddharma Pundarika,* most assuredly is, one parable given therein,[30] as an illustration of the Eternal Buddha's willingness to resort to any method or devise, in order to get mankind out of the "burning house," outrages all sense of the essential righteousness of the Eternal. Modern Japanese Buddhism, with all its adaptation and by this very fact, appears in the light of seeking through whatever means possible to disguise the essentially bitter character of its fruit. When all is said and done, the fruits of whatever Abiding Presence Buddhism may have to offer have not compared favorably with the fruits of the Spirit of Christ which Paul describes as "love, joy, peace, long-suffering, kindness, goodness, faithfulness, meekness, self-

control."[31] A comparison on one of these qualities is illuminating: although kindness or mercy
is perhaps the one quality of the noble life on
which Buddhism places largest emphasis, it
must be admitted that as manifested in hospitals, asylums, schools for unfortunates, me-
dical centers, charity establishments, etc., the
Buddhists though constituting 80% of the population and with almost 1500 years of history
and opportunity in Japan have failed to produce the fruits of mercy and kindness which
Christianity has to its credit in less than 75
years of service and with only one-half of one
percent of the population acknowledging dis-
cipleship.

The Japanese are not unresponsive to such
evidences of the indwelling spirit of the Christian God. Indeed, their hearts go out to such
demonstrations as proof of the sincerity and
vitality of one's religious faith. It is significant
what ready response they make to such forms
of service as those of the Red Cross, social settlements, charity and welfare work, and the
like. It is also significant what a large percent-
age of the leaders even in civic movements of
this nature are Christians, and how few are devout Buddhists, or Shintoists, or Confucianists.
It would appear that, except as the Japanese
have consciously or unconsciously drawn from
Palistinian wells, they have failed to find in their

draughts of Buddhist, Shinto and Confucian refreshment the quality of the "living water" of which Jesus spoke. Let us therefore look briefly at this Source of the Christian's inspiration and ability to transform society while at the same time saving himself and others to eternal life. And let us seek to discover to what extent Jesus Christ has been vouchsafed to the Japanese both as Ideal and as Power for the realization of ideals in every-day life.

G. THE PLACE OF JESUS CHRIST IN THE RELIGIOUS LIFE OF JAPAN TODAY

It is reasonable to suppose that we should find no great appreciation of a doctrinal Christ today in Japan or in any other non-Christian land. Jesus seldom made his approach to Galilean fishermen and tax-gatherers in that way, and it is unlikely that he would do so among present day Japanese fishermen and tax-gatherers. We have, however seen one ardent Shinto scholar, Dr. G. Kato, so impressed with the child-like faith of the Emperor Meiji in the Providence of a Christ-like God as to exclaim, "It is owing to this view of theism that Christ could see the glory of God revealed even in a lily and in a falling sparow."[32] Again, we are assured by one of Japan's greatest legal spirits, an almost fanatical Shintoist, that "It is by all means necessary to appreciate the essence of the spirit

of Jesus himself and to save and develop this by
means of the great spirit of Shinto."[33] Similarly,
we have observed a willingness among sincere
Buddhists to recognize the lofty place of Jesus
among the world's spiritual leaders and to in-
clude him, if possible, among the Buddhas, even
as Roman Christianity has canonized Gautama
as St. Josephat.[34] Dr. Anesaki in a treatise,
"Let there be Light," written some years ago,
boldly shows how Buddhism and Christianity
start from opposite poles of thought and yet
arrive at the same end so far as popular results
are concerned; i.e. they converge in faith in a
great life. There is no hesitation on the part of
this distinguished Buddhist to picture the life of
Christ in its fullest significance and beauty;
one wonders whether even the Oriental scholar
is not, perforce, drawn to Jesus rather than to
Buddha, and then falls into rationalized com-
parisons.

Again, it is common knowledge that a Hon-
gwanji temple in the Kwansai region near Kyo-
to includes among its most precious treasures an
ancient and worn copy of the New Testament.
Many Buddhist priests frankly admit deriving
inspiration from study of the life of Christ. It
is not unusual at all to find them in Bible classes
conducted by missionaries. Dr. Armstrong re-
lates the conversion of two priests by the example of Jesus' life among men.[35] Indeed, there

are numerous cases of such transfers of loyalty among Confucian, Shinto and Buddhist believers to the person and fellowship of Christ. Pictures and stories from the life of Jesus, with exposition, appear in many government textbooks for school use and in teachers' manuals. A Japanese non-Christian actor a few years ago gave an interpretation of the Life of Jesus in Tokyo's most famous theatre, the house being thronged throughout the rather long run of the play, and newspapers commenting upon the observed effect upon the public. Students, responding to that which called the youthful Jesus to the Galilean road as teacher and prophet, go out likewise in the mild afternoons and evenings in Japan to proclaim the Jesus-way, and Sunday schools are found in almost every village and hamlet. Churches—some well-filled, some not so favored—dot the empire, and Christ is also preached from hundreds of homes in communities where there are yet no churches. Christian kindergartens and schools, as well as institutions for the blind, the lepers, the orphans, the infirm, also give constant testimony to the deep impression which Jesus has made upon Japanese life.

To Christians these evidences of the Jesus-outlook constitute the highest values in the religious culture of the Japanese people.   Complemented as they must be by all the indigenous values heretofore enumerated, they promise most for the future growth and development of this alert Oriental nation, and for the advancement of that state of world-fellowship and mutual helpfulness to which Christians refer when speaking of the Kingdom of God on Earth. Again, it seems to us that only from these particular values can that Divine purpose be realized to which we refer as the Kingdom of Heaven, and in which so much depends upon the character and nature of That which is worshipped as Divine. We see light and love and hope ahead only as Japan and all the nations of the world discover, each for itself and in its own way, that all-prevading all-transcending Spirit which to Jesus was Father and God. We are not in any sense inclined to dictate to the Japanese how He shall or should appear to their Oriental eyes. Still, we cannot believe He can be to them most awe-inspiring, most righteous, most inclusive, most purposeful, and at the same time most intimate and friendly, if less than Personal, Loving and Eternal, even as Jesus insisted. This conception in turn implies His appreciation of true worth in the personalities of His creatures and a sensitiveness to the yearnings He himself has placed within us. Hence, He must have for His children a scheme of salvation through which, if freely chosen, they may bring their lives to fullest richness of meaning and to highest fruition of purpose, approximating thereby His plan for our lives and a likeness to the character of Jesus Our Lord.

As to the long future we can only fall back upon the inadequacies of mere words to express sublime intuitions and deepest convictions: "Henceforth there is laid up for me a crown of righteousness which the Lord, the righteous judge, shall give me at that day; and not for me only but also to all who have loved his appearing."[36] If such a faith be egoism, it is the most sublimated egotism in the pages of either literature or history, and Jesus is both its foundation and its epiphany. A universe which can produce such a faith, and such a life as that of Jesus founded thereupon, reveals therein its highest meaning and purpose.

CONCLUSION

We have thus far been seeking to discover and to set forth certain elements of genuine value in the religious culture of the Japanese people. We have not concerned ourselves with the valueless, the temporary, the unideal, the vicious elements therein, however obvious they may have seemed. We are perfectly aware that perhaps for every favorable reaction to the various phases of the religious life of the Japanese, one or more unfavorable criticism could just as truthfully be made. It is as apparent to the writer as to any other critic of Oriental life that Shinto, Confucianism and Buddhism have all failed to lift the Japanese to as exalted a level of personal and social life as they are capable of attaining. Moreover, we have no desire to ignore the tragic shortcomings of Westernized and institutional Christianity as it has been preached and practiced both during the earliest Catholic efforts at evangelization in Japan, and in more recent decades. Nevertheless, we have the utmost faith in the ability of essential Christianity to accomplish that wherein all these less than Christ-like agencies have failed. This conviction and a desire to assist in that consummation constitute the sole justification for the writer's present efforts.

Christianity as an institution may not have met with the degree of success in Japan to which sanguine prophets looked forward a generation ago. Organized Christianity is held in indifferent and even contemptuous regard by altogether too many, serious minded and influential Japanese to permit of a highly optimistic prognostication for the immediate future. Yet, there are unmistakable grounds for the presumption that, even though the Church as such should fail to maintain the gains it has already realized in Japan, still Christianity in some form will succeed. Just as the Religion of Jesus took the ascendancy over the numerous less vital religions of Syria, Asia Minor, Greece, Rome, and Northern Europe in its Westward advance, so *in essence* is it destined to make conquest of every less ideal and less potent faith and philosophy in its much retarded penetration of the East. The Christianity which succeeded in Asia Minor and Greece was not the exact faith which triumphed in the Roman Empire; neither was the Christian faith which finally established itself in Germany, the Scandinavian lands and Great Britain identical with that of Rome. Rather does it seem that these were in large respects different religious systems, yet with a common nucleus of faith and hope in Christ and in His Father-God. To account for this we have but to observe that in these diverse cultural backgrounds there were certain vital elements which had not existed, or at least were not dominant, in the culture from which the new faith came to them. These newly encountered values demanded recognition, and, receiving it, sometimes all too grudgingly, proceeded to identify themselves with Christianity in new and popular and indigenous forms.

It is not unnatural that Christianity should similarly adapt itself to Japanese culture and to religious values already existing therein. Not infrequently does one hear the criticism of Christian missionaries that they have cared little for genuine values in cultural and religious backgrounds outside their own particular systems, and that they have only sought indiscriminately to destroy the old institutions in order that completely new might arise in their stead. This, however, is not in keeping with the best in the history of Christian advance through two thousand years, nor with the method of Jesus who sought "not to destroy but to fulfill."[1] The truest and greatest advances of the Christian faith and culture have been accomplished in this latter spirit. The expansion of Christendom has been a story of continuous adaptation to new and challenging situations. Where these changes have been for the sake of recognizing and accepting new and genuine values, the

Church has been strengthened and blessed.
Where the accommodations have involved a re-
linquishing of Christianity's lofty ideals, the ad-
vantages, if any, have been temporary and retribution swift. There are both encouragement
and warning in the story of Buddhism's adaptation to the conditions encountered in its progress
from India Northward and Eastward; encouragement in that, as we have seen, Mahayana
Buddhism was constantly evolving a more positive theology and a higher regard for personality, until it approximated in the teachings of
certain sects the Christian view of life; warning, in that willingness to compromise its distinctive moral ideals invariably resulted in
degeneration and disgrace.

Let the Christianizing forces in the Orient
continue to profit by both the errors and the
triumphs of the past. Only by such conscious
alertness have the followers of Jesus achieved
their greatest victories. So shall they also continue to make conquest of men's loyalties. It is
this form of an evolving and gloriously growing
Christianity of which Dr. Ernst Troeltsch failed
to take account in the conclusions of his declin-
ing years, that each of the world's racial groups
possesses "a religion which has grown up with
them and from which they cannot sever themselves."[2]   Even after recounting how Christianity by adaptation and growth became a typ-

ically European faith to meet European conditions, and differing here and there, according to cultural backgrounds, Professor Troeltsch refused to see how the spirit and outlook of Christ may in like manner so integrate themselves as to exactly meet the needs of as yet non-Christian peoples; with the result that Oriental lands may accept a form of Christianity differing as much or more from the European, as the various types of organized Christianity in Europe differ among themselves, and all differing from the form of the faith in the first few centuries of Our Lord's era.

That a religion may be transported and, while being greatly altered by accommodation, may yet mould another civilization into conformity with its essential ideals, is clearly evident in the history of Buddhism in Japan. The great changes in Japanese civilization brought about by the influence of this foreign religion through fifteen hundred years have been considerably more than "little shiftings . . . . . at the fringes," which is all that Dr. Troeltsch can concede as the probable effect of an imported faith upon a strong, indigenous culture.[3]

The effect accomplished by Christian influence upon Japan in but a few decades also discounts the Troeltsch thesis. One big factor Dr. Troeltsch failed to take into account was the possibility of a backward nation suddenly awakening to new life and setting out to transform itself into a realm more in keeping with the culture and scientific atmosphere of the modern world, as Japan has done in the past seventy years. Would Professor Troeltsch not have recognized the need of a new moral and religious life to meet the problems of such new economic and social conditions? He seems not to have considered this phase of the matter at all. What he was mightily concerned with was that it be recognized that "a religion in the several forms assumed by it always depends upon the intellectual, social and national conditions among which it exists,"[4] and that "other racial groups living under entirely different cultural conditions may experience their contacts with the divine life in quite a different way."[5] Another of Dr. Troeltsch's observations is especially good: "Always remember that the religion thus adapted by another people will individualize itself anew."[6]

All this is true, and is just what we have been trying to demonstrate in the foregoing pages. But, from Dr. Troeltsch's viewpoint, it proves too much. Granted that Christianity may be permitted to adapt and "individualize" itself in the Orient as it has done in the West, and as Buddhism and other faiths have likewise done in lands other than their birthplaces — a possi-